Faith in Education

Faith in Education

The role of the churches in education:
a response to the Dearing Report on
church schools in the third millennium

John Burn
John Marks
Peter Pilkington
Penny Thompson

Foreword by
Brian Griffiths

Civitas: Institute for the Study of Civil Society
London

First published September 2001

© The Institute for the Study of Civil Society 2001
The Mezzanine, Elizabeth House
39 York Road, London SE1 7NQ
email: books@civitas.org.uk

ISBN 1-903 386-14-4

Typeset by Civitas
in New Century Schoolbook

Printed in Great Britain by
The Cromwell Press
Trowbridge, Wiltshire

When there was no education, Church schools led the way till the nation followed; now that there is bad education, it is for the Church schools again to lead.

Samuel Barnett, 1885

Contents

	Page
Authors	vii
Foreword *Lord Griffiths of Fforestfach*	ix
Introduction *John Marks*	1
Standards in Church of England, Roman Catholic and LEA Schools in England *John Marks*	5

Church Schools:
    A Critique of Much Current Practice
    John Burn
	37

The Church in Education *Peter Pilkington*	51

How the Will of Parliament on Religious
    Education was Diluted by Civil Servants
    and the Religious Education Profession
    Penny Thompson
	57

Notes	74

Authors

John Burn is now an educational consultant with a particular interest in Christian education. He is chairman of the Christian Institute, a national organisation based in the North East of England. For almost 20 years he was the headmaster of two large urban comprehensive schools, one of which was Emmanuel College, Gateshead, one of the first of the 15 city technology colleges in England. He was a member of a number of significant national committees including the National Curriculum Council, the Schools Curriculum and Assessment Authority and the Council for the Accreditation of Teacher Education. He was also a member of the Archbishop of Canterbury's Commission on Urban Priority Areas which produced the report *Faith in the City* in 1985. He is a lay reader in the Church of England and has been a magistrate for the past 26 years. He is vice chairman of the directors of Emmanuel College, Gateshead and is a director of two independent Christian schools, Hamilton College near Glasgow and Grindon Hall, Sunderland.

John Marks is director of the Civitas Education Unit and co-director, with Baroness Cox, of the Educational Research Trust. He was formerly administrator of the National Council for Educational Standards (NCES) and has over 40 years of teaching experience in universities, polytechnics and schools. He was a member of the Schools Examination and Assessment Council, 1990-3, the National Curriculum Council, 1992-3, and the Schools Curriculum & Assessment Authority, 1993-1997. He is currently vice chairman of the governors of a comprehensive school, having first been elected as a parent governor in 1978. His many publications on education include: *Standards in Schools: Assessment, Accountability and the Purpose of Education* (The Social Market Foundation, 1991); *Value for Money in Education: Opportunity Costs and the Relationship between Standards and Resources* (Campaign for Real Education, 1992);

Vocational Education, Training and Qualifications in Britain (Institute of Economic Affairs, 1996); *Standards of English & Maths in Primary Schools for 1995* (Social Market Foundation, 1996); *Standards of Arithmetic: How to Correct the Decline* (Centre for Policy Studies, 1996); *Standards of Reading, Spelling & Maths for 7-year-olds in Primary Schools for 1995* (Social Market Foundation, 1997); *A Selective or Comprehensive System: Which Works Best? The Empirical Evidence* (Centre for Policy Studies, 1998); *An Anatomy of Failure: Standards in English Schools for 1997* (Social Market Foundation, 1998); *Value for Money in LEA Schools* (Centre for Policy Studies, 1998); *What are Special Educational Needs?; An Analysis of a New Growth Industry* (Centre for Policy Studies, July, 2000); *The Betrayed Generations: Standards in British Schools 1950-2000* (Centre for Policy Studies, 2001) and *Girls Know Better: Educational Attainments of Boys and Girls* (Civitas, 2001).

Peter Pilkington taught in Tanganyika from 1955-57, and was ordained in 1959. He taught at Eton from 1962-75, was headmaster of King's School, Canterbury from 1975-86, and High Master of St Paul's School from 1986-92. He was an honorary canon of Canterbury Cathedral from 1975-90, and is now canon emeritus. He has been chairman of the Broadcasting Complaints Commission since 1992, and was created Baron Pilkington of Oxenford in 1995.

Penny Thompson has taught religious education in comprehensive schools for 15 years and has always had an interest in the theory of the subject. She is an Anglican. She is now a part-time teacher at an independent school and is engaged in research for a book which will argue the case for religious education to be based on the truth of a particular religion. She has written numerous articles and reviews in professional journals. She has also written a series of five occasional papers on the topic of religious education. These have been published as booklets and are available on her web-site: www.angelfire.com/pe/pennyt/

Foreword

The Dearing Report *The Way Ahead: Church of England Schools in the New Millennium* is a landmark publication on the place of the Church of England in primary and secondary education in this country. It was commissioned by the Archbishops' Council with the terms of reference 'to review the achievements of Church of England schools and to make proposals for their future development'. A consultation report was published in December 2000 to which the scale of the response was 'almost overwhelming but encouraging'.[1] The report, which is vintage Dearing, thorough, balanced and well argued, covers all aspects of the subject and puts forward no less than 79 recommendations, with clusters of recommendations directed variously at the Archbishops' Council, dioceses, parishes and deaneries, schools and school governors, church colleges, theological colleges, courses and schemes, the Church of England Board of Education, the National Society, government and government agencies.

The report is based on three key assumptions: that the demand for places in church schools far exceeds existing provision; that in some important cities such as Newcastle, Norwich, Plymouth, Sunderland and Sheffield, there are no maintained Church of England secondary schools; and that church schools are at the heart of the Church's mission to the nation. In response to such under-provision, the most eye-catching proposal of the report is an increase in the number of places in church schools equivalent to creating an extra 100 secondary schools over the next seven years, something which would require the Church to raise £25 million over this period. The government in its green paper on schools, published in February this year,[2] has already welcomed working in partnership with the Church on these proposals, as have the two other main political parties.

The Dearing Report provides a unique opportunity for the Church of England to make a significant contribution to improving the spiritual, moral and academic opportunities for children in this country. It is because of this that all contributors to this volume welcome its publication. But in their contributions they also recognise the considerable challenges faced in implementing the report's recommendations. In some cases they hint of difficulties, in others they question whether the report is bold enough. The report raises four main questions which need to be addressed, namely: what constitutes the distinctiveness of a church school; the meaning of partnership between the Church and government in primary and secondary education; the training and recruitment of Christian teachers; and the issue of resources and funding.

Before we develop these main themes, two points need to be made. One is that, although academic standards in church schools are somewhat higher than in LEA schools, average standards in church schools are significantly below expected achievement at ages 11 and 14. John Marks, with his usual high standard of statistical analysis, points out that, even though academic performance in church schools is slightly higher than in LEA schools, there are 'staggeringly large variations in standards between church schools' (p. 27). Church schools may be oversubscribed but the Church still faces a huge task in raising standards in its schools. The second point is that before we explore the four main issues already mentioned, the report also has a good deal to say on many other issues, such as the relationship between church schools in the maintained sector and the independent sector; the responsibilities of parish clergy, especially in their training, if the proposals are to work; the need to reduce the administrative burden on heads of small primary schools, a good number of which are to be found in rural areas; and the contrast between the Roman Catholic and Anglican approaches to education over the past 50 years. All of these are far from unimportant issues but not central to the major thrust of the report.

In terms of the major themes, the report goes out of its way to emphasise that church schools should be distinctively and recognisably Christian institutions. In this sense the report has a refreshingly spiritual emphasis. It quotes with approval one diocese which said in evidence that Christian values and principles should 'run through every area of school life as the writing runs through a stick of rock'.[3] The church school is a community of faith which provides a spiritual and moral basis for the development of the whole person and 'a sure foundation for personal and social values based on the person and ministry of Christ'.[4] At the same time the approach is distinctively Anglican rather than Roman Catholic or that of independent evangelical schools.

In practice, an Anglican approach has two important implications: first that Church of England voluntary aided schools will have an admissions policy open to all who live in the parish, including people of other faiths and no faith; and second, that the Church will not use the school to proselytise. At the same time, for a church school to be a distinctively Christian institution it must have a Christian core. What precisely should be included in this core is a matter for debate. At a minimum, the report suggests that the head teacher should be committed to maintaining the Christian character of the school in its day-to-day activities and in the curriculum; that there should be a real act of Christian worship every day; that RE should take up at least five per cent of school time; that the character and quality of religious education should be of particular concern to the head teacher and governing body; that the school observes the Christian festivals; that school life incorporates the values of the Christian faith (with special emphasis given to creating an ethos of honesty, openness, cultural and ethnic diversity and forgiveness); that the school teaches how to pray and the liturgy and that it maintains an active relationship with the parish church.[5]

All of this is a far cry from the Durham Report of 1970 which attempted to play down the distinctiveness of Christian schools. In this sense the Dearing Report is a huge step forward. But one cannot help concluding that the report is stronger in emphasising the school as a liturgical community rather than as a learning and teaching institution concerned with Christian truth. It would be quite unfair to suggest that the report pays no attention to the matter of curriculum. It does. But it does so in a vague way, lacking the sharpness with which it tackles other areas. As John Burn, a head teacher with a successful track record of running Christian schools, puts it, the report seems reluctant to spell out the importance of the schools teaching orthodox Christian belief and practice. More generally, the report has opened up a debate as to what are the essential requirements for a church school to be a vital Christian institution, while recognising at the same time that schools in different communities will find they have to respond to the distinctive needs of their catchment areas. While not changing its basic approach to education, the Anglican Church may still have much to learn from the Roman Catholic Church and schools with a conservative evangelical foundation, of what constitutes a distinctively Christian institution.

With Lord Dearing as Chairman, the issue of partnership is, as might be imagined, dealt with sensitively. Nevertheless, it remains an extremely difficult area. By advocating the creation of 100 new secondary schools, a change where possible from voluntary controlled to voluntary aided status, and the creation of city academies, the Church may well find that its partnership with central government is strengthened. But in this new contract between the Church and the state, it is the local education authorities who may perceive themselves as losing out. An increase in aided schools and city academies will reduce the power of the LEAs. Typically, LEAs tend to be suspicious that church schools, because they are oversubscribed, and whether intending it or not, are using admissions policy as a form of selection, something which might well be in conflict with the LEA's own plans for the area. In view of the close historic relationship between diocesan boards of education and local education authorities, the latter may offer resistance to some of the proposals in this report, and not surprisingly attract sympathy from the Church of England bureaucracy. The report is at pains to point out that any attempt to implement its proposals is only possible with the explicit consent of the local community and that the expansion of provision by the Church must be in partnership with the LEAs. Canon Peter Pilkington observes, however, that in the past the Church has tended to accept the educational policy drawn up by government, both local and national (p. 56). It may be that the report, in wishing to place such a strong emphasis on both consent and partnership, will find that the price it pays is a dilution in the distinctiveness of its schools as Christian institutions.

The third theme relates to the training and recruitment of Christian teachers, which the report rightly sees as crucial to the development of Christian schools. Ensuring that there are a sufficient number of Christian teachers to staff the expansion of Christian schools is *the* major problem facing the implementation of the Dearing Report, and it has three components. Any serious overall shortage of teachers such as exists at present is likely to be reflected in staffing problems in all schools, including church schools. The Church therefore has a major incentive to ensure that teachers are far better compensated than at present and that they are supported, especially on disciplinary issues, more than they sometimes appear to be. Next, there is the Church's challenge to confront its members with the vocation of teaching. It is all too easy in an individualist and materialist society for Christian students to think of vocation in a secular framework and ignore the ideal of service which is at the heart of the gospel. This is a major challenge, especially for the clergy in communicating to their churches the meaning of vocation. Finally, even if Christians opt for a teaching career, they may well find that, because church colleges have become so secular, after they have completed a course they lack a proper understanding of orthodox Christian teaching and have been left ill-equipped to develop a Christian mind or world-view, which is of relevance to all aspects of school life, particularly the curriculum.

This is a major problem facing the Church as a whole, and especially those parts of the Church which are growing most rapidly, namely the charismatic and evangelical churches, from which one would expect to draw a significant number of students entering teaching. At present, there is an insufficient sense of vocation associated with a career of teaching in church schools to draw younger people into the profession.

The final and inevitable subject raised by the report is the finance needed to fund this expansion, something which is not dealt with by the contributors to this volume and which, even in the report, is dealt with fairly briefly. The report attaches a figure of £25 million to its proposals (excluding the cost of establishing the new city academies), though it also says, in a disarming manner, 'it could be decidedly more'.[6] Because of the Anglican emphasis on the church school serving the whole community, it should certainly be possible for the Church to raise this sum, though I suspect a good deal will depend on making the appeal or appeals relevant to local needs, in particular to show parents and local employers the way in which their contributions should be viewed as an investment in their own children and in their communities. While I believe the money can be raised, we should not underestimate Canon Pilkington's comment on the achievement of the Roman Catholic church in increasing secondary schools six-fold since 1950, namely that it took a great sacrifice (p. 55).

Lord Dearing has presented a visionary report of how the Church of England can serve the needs of children, their families and their communities in this country in the new millennium through creating more church schools and strengthening existing ones. He rightly emphasises the particular role his proposals might play in disadvantaged communities. If it is to be realised, it will clearly require a sacrifice on the Church's part, as well as a return to a more orthodox understanding and teaching of the Christian faith. If we fail to implement the report however, we will forever and rightly stand accused by a future generation of failure to act responsibly as trustees of our Christian heritage.

Lord Griffiths of Fforestfach

Introduction

John Marks

The chapters in this book are intended as a commentary on the Report of the Church Schools Review Group set up by the Archbishops' Council of the Church of England and chaired by Lord Dearing.[1] At the same time, they provide much essential background information—both historical and current—and make suggestions which take further the arguments of the Dearing committee. They are intended to have at least two purposes:

- to commend and to complement the Dearing proposals

- to try to illuminate the debate about the future of church schools in the twenty-first century.

The first chapter, 'Standards in Church of England, Roman Catholic and LEA schools in England' by John Marks, presents data for the standards achieved by pupils at all Church of England, Roman Catholic and local education authority (LEA) schools in the whole country.[2]

Overall standards are poor, with the extent of under-achievement increasing substantially for older pupils, and this is just as much the case for Church of England and Roman Catholic schools as it is for LEA schools. Average standards in church schools are a little higher than in LEA schools and their pupils' rates of progress are also a little higher so that their advantage over LEA schools increases for older pupils. In summary, pupils at church schools, both Church of England and Roman Catholic, are, on average, ahead of pupils at LEA schools by about three months of progress at the age of seven, by about six months of progress at the age of 11, and from six to ten months by the age of 14. Nevertheless average standards in church schools are significantly below expectations at the ages of 11 and 14.

1

However, this relatively favourable average performance nationally is overshadowed by the staggeringly large variations in average standards between schools. It is very disturbing that, even at the age of seven, many schools of all kinds are behind the standards that they are expected to reach, particularly since the expected standard at this age is relatively undemanding.[3] By 11, even more schools have fallen even further behind, and by 14, there are large numbers of church as well as LEA schools where pupils are three or more years behind in both English and mathematics.

These enormous differences are likely to be due to similar causes in church schools as the ones found in LEA schools. The main considerations are:

- differential effectiveness of different teaching methods, especially in the early teaching of reading and arithmetic

- over-reliance on mixed ability grouping as opposed to setting by ability

- superior performance of selective or specialised schools compared with all-ability schools

- differential effectiveness of different philosophies of education, arguments over which have bedevilled education policy in this country for at least three decades.[4]

Therefore, in addition to encouraging the Church of England to expand the number of its schools, and its secondary schools in particular, the Dearing committee should urge the Church not to abdicate its responsibilities for standards, as it has all too often done in the recent past, in deference to prevailing lay educational opinion. Instead, the church should investigate what is and has been happening and make its own views known on the absolutely fundamental matter of standards, which should be of major concern to all involved in the education of the next generation.

The second chapter, 'Church Schools: A critique of much current practice' by John Burn, gives a personal account of how two academically very successful state comprehensive schools were run by a headmaster who is a committed

Christian. He describes how the distinctively Christian ethos which he and his staff were able to instil in their schools played a central role in both the academic and the pastoral success of the schools. He goes on to suggest that the future for church schools lies in developing such a distinctively Christian ethos and in providing an education which is different from that available in non-church schools. He deals in particular with:

- Christian worship
- the relationship between religious education and good citizenship
- other important moral issues including sex and relationship education.

The chapter ends by making proposals which would help church schools to recruit, train and retain Christian teachers.

In the third chapter, 'The Church in Education' by Canon Peter Pilkington, the author writes from the point of view of an Anglican clergyman, and a distinguished historian and headmaster. He reviews briefly the history of the Church's role in education and discusses in particular the way in which the National Society moved away in the 1970s from a Christian distinctiveness in the education which it provided and how it is now trying to regain that distinctiveness.

Canon Pilkington welcomes this attempt as he does the major recommendations of the Dearing review and makes some pertinent suggestions as to how they might be developed further and put into practice.

In the final chapter, 'How the Will of Parliament on Religious Education was Diluted by Civil Servants and the Religious Education Profession', Penny Thompson describes how assurances given in Parliament about the nature of religious education in schools required by the 1988 Education Reform Act—without which the Act would not have become law—have been overturned by the combined efforts of civil servants and of some leaders of the religious education profession. Penny Thompson establishes that the real meaning of the law has been obscured so successfully that few know it and fewer still attempt to follow it. This needs to be exposed so that those responsible for religious education in state schools know what the real intention of the law was and can begin to provide a different sort of religious education: one that proceeds from a particular faith, thus laying the foundations for real spiritual growth. This needs to be pursued by the Church of England as a matter of urgency, because it is entirely consonant with its moves towards a more specifically Christian distinctiveness in the education which it provides in its own schools.

Overall, we hope that the Church of England and other authorities will respond to these diverse comments, commentaries and suggestions in the constructive spirit in which they are made.

Standards in Church of England, Roman Catholic and LEA Schools in England

John Marks

This introductory chapter provides a brief analysis of the results achieved by church and other schools as indicated by national curriculum test results at seven, 11 & 14 and by GCSE results at 16 and A-level results at 18. Results are compared for Church of England schools, Roman Catholic schools and LEA (community) schools.

A. *Introduction*

There are enormous variations in standards from school to school—even with schools of the same type in similar areas. This is true at all ages for which we have national information:

- at 7, 11 and 14 in national curriculum tests
- at 16 in public examination results for GCSE and vocational qualifications
- at 18 in A-level and GNVQ results and in access to higher education.

As pupils get older the variations in standards increase. The result is that there are great differences in achievements and opportunities for pupils from different backgrounds and areas.

This is just as true of church schools as it is of other schools, as this chapter will show.

This paper summarises the available information about current standards in church schools in this country and compares them with standards in LEA community schools.

It covers standards in English and mathematics in primary and secondary schools at the ages of seven, 11 and 14; and general GCSE results at the age of 16 together with some information about A-level results at 18.[1]

Current Standards in basic subjects at Key Stages 1, 2 & 3 (Primary Schools at seven and 11 and Secondary Schools at 14)

Figure 1 and Figures 3 to 8 (pp. 18-23) are distribution charts which show the standards reached by pupils at the ages of seven (Key Stage 1), 11 (Key Stage 2) and 14 (Key Stage 3). For example Figure 1 shows the standards reached in reading, derived from national curriculum tests, by seven-year-old pupils at all primary schools in England.[2]

Figure 1
Average reading 'subject age' of seven-year-old pupils in individual schools in England

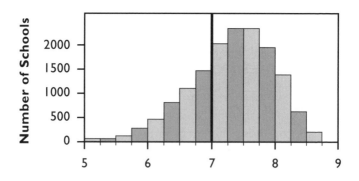

The horizontal axis shows the average 'subject age' for reading for individual schools; the vertical axis shows the number of schools.[3] The dark vertical line on such charts indicates the average real chronological age of the pupils.

Thus, for example, there are about 2,000 state schools whose seven-year-old pupils have average 'reading ages' between seven years and seven years three months but only about 600 state schools whose seven-year-old pupils have average 'reading ages' between eight years three months and eight years six months.[4]

Summary of National Standards at 7, 11 and 14

Overall standards are low; the average standard achieved by pupils at 11 and 14 is significantly below the standard they should reach for their ages.

The shortfall between actual standards and expected standards increases for older pupils. At the age of seven they are, on average, a little ahead of expected standards but by 11 they are about a year behind and by 14 two years behind.

The spread between the standards of different schools of the same type is very large indeed. It increases from about 2.5 years at age seven (the range of 'subject ages' is from about six to 8.5 years) to nearly four years at age 11 (from about 8.25 to 11.75 years) to five years or more at age 14 (from about nine or less to 14 or more years).

The results for reading/English and for mathematics are very similar at all ages, with average standards being marginally higher in mathematics.

Current Standards In GCSE: %5A*C In Individual Schools

Figure 2 shows the distribution for the percentage of pupils gaining five or more GCSE grades A* to C (%5A*C) in all comprehensive secondary schools in the country. Figures 9-11 (pp. 24-26) show similar distributions for GCSE and A-level results for other kinds of secondary school.

In such distribution charts, the horizontal axis shows %5A*C or some other measure of academic performance; the vertical axis shows the number of schools; the dark vertical line indicates the national average for the particular category of school.

Thus, for example, in Figure 2 there are nearly 300 comprehensive schools with between 40 per cent and 45 per cent of pupils gaining five or more GCSE grades A* to C, and another 300 with between 45 per cent and 50 per cent.

However, only about 100 comprehensive schools had between 65 per cent and 70 per cent of pupils in this category.

The distribution for all comprehensive schools is very broad—almost uniform between 20 per cent and 60 per cent with many schools both above and below these figures. Many comprehensive schools thus have five or six times fewer pupils obtaining five or more GCSE passes at Grades A*C than other comprehensive schools; more detailed analyses show that differences on this scale exist even for schools in the same or similar areas.

Figure 2
*%5A*C GCSE for Comprehensive Schools in England*

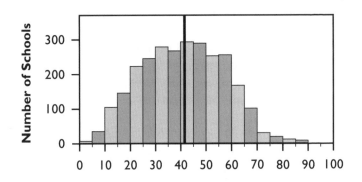

B. Numbers Of Schools And Average Standards For Church And LEA Schools

Numbers of Primary Schools (Tables 1 and 2)

Just over a quarter of all primary schools are Church of England schools, just over ten per cent are Roman Catholic schools and about two thirds are LEA schools.

Average Standards at 7 (Table 1)

Pupils at church schools, both Church of England and Roman Catholic, are, on average, about three months ahead of pupils at LEA schools for both reading and mathematics. All primary schools are achieving, on average, a little above the expectation for their age for both reading and mathematics.

Table 1
Age 7 (Key Stage 1) - Primary Schools

Type of School	No. of Schools	Reading Age	Mathematics Age
LEA	9,542	7.29	7.38
Church of England	4,182	7.59	7.59
Roman Catholic	1,640	7.63	7.60

Average Standards at 11 (Table 2)
In both English and mathematics, 11-year-old pupils at both Church of England and Roman Catholic schools are about six months of progress ahead of pupils at LEA schools. Pupils at Roman Catholic schools achieve slightly better results than pupils at Church of England schools. However, all pupils are substantially below expectations for their age—approximately eight months behind for church schools and about a year behind for LEA schools.

Table 2
Age 11 (Key Stage 2) - Primary Schools

Type of School	No. of Schools	English Age	Mathematics Age
LEA	8,506	10.06	9.91
Church of England	3,751	10.49	10.32
Roman Catholic	1,612	10.65	10.40

Progress from 7 to 11 (Table 3)
Progress made, on average, for pupils at all types of school between the ages of seven and 11 is significantly less than

expectations. Pupils at LEA schools make, on average, just over two and a half years of progress in four years—only about two thirds of the progress that is expected. Pupils at church schools make, on average, progress of nearly three years between seven and 11—that is about 75 per cent of expectations.

Table 3
Years of progress from 7 to 11

Type of School	Years of Progress Reading/English	Years of Progress Mathematics
LEA	2.77	2.53
Church of England	2.90	2.73
Roman Catholic	3.02	2.80

Numbers of Secondary Schools (Tables 4 & 6)

Church of England schools comprise just under five per cent of all secondary schools while Roman Catholic schools make up about 11 per cent of all secondary schools. The rest are LEA schools except for a very small number of religious schools from other denominations. There are thus very similar proportions of Roman Catholic secondary schools as compared with primary schools but significantly fewer Church of England secondary schools—only about five per cent compared with 25 per cent for primary schools.

Average Standards at 14 (Table 4)

In English, pupils at Church of England and Roman Catholic schools are each about nine or ten months ahead of pupils at LEA schools. In mathematics the differences are slightly smaller with pupils at church schools being, on average, about six months ahead of those at LEA schools. Even so, all pupils are, on average, achieving substantially below expectations for their age—pupils at church schools are about 15 months in progress behind and pupils in LEA schools are about two years behind.

Table 4
Age 14 (Key Stage 3) - Secondary Schools

Type of School	No. of Schools	English Age	Mathematics Age
LEA	2,411	11.90	12.23
Church of England	136	12.66	12.81
Roman Catholic	336	12.75	12.67

Progress from 11-14 (Table 5)

It is difficult to relate results at 14 to those at 11 because it is not always clear that pupils who were in church primary schools will necessarily go on to church secondary schools. This is particularly the case for Church of England schools which, as we have seen, have many fewer places available for secondary pupils than they do for primary-age pupils. Bearing these caveats in mind, Table 5 shows the numbers of years of progress for pupils between 11 and 14.

Table 5
Years of progress from 11 to 14

Type of School	Years of Progress English	Years of Progress Mathematics
LEA	1.84	2.32
Church of England	2.17	2.49
Roman Catholic	2.10	2.27

On average, pupils at LEA schools make just under two years of progress in three years in English, while pupils at church schools make just over two years of progress in three years in English. They are thus making only about two-thirds of progress which is expected. In mathematics pupils at LEA schools and Roman Catholic schools make, on average, about two years and four months of progress in three years, while those at Church of England schools make about two years and six months of progress. All pupils are therefore progressing at only about three-quarters of the rate expected.

Average Standards at 16 (Table 6)

It is not possible to present progress from 11 to 16 or from 14 to 16 in the easily understandable way that we have been able to do for the ages of 7, 11 and 14. This is because the grades in 16-plus examination are not capable of being expressed in the same way as national curriculum test results. Instead we will look at three measures of GCSE performance which are all used in National Performance Tables.

Table 6
Age 16 (GCSE) - Secondary Schools

Type of School	No. of Schools	%5+A*C	Points/ Pupil	% of pupils achieving no GCSE passes A* - G
LEA	2,434	42.70	35.80	5.10
Church of England	139	51.20	40.20	4.00
Roman Catholic	338	48.90	39.60	3.80

Pupils Achieving Five or More Grades A to C at GCSE*

51.2 per cent of pupils at Church of England schools obtain five or more grades A* to C at GCSE compared with 48.9 per cent at Roman Catholic schools and 42.7 per cent at LEA schools. This is an advantage of about 20 per cent for Church of England schools and 15 per cent for Roman Catholic schools compared with LEA schools.

GCSE Points[5] Per Pupil

Pupils at Church of England schools obtain, on average, 40.2 GCSE points per pupil compared with 39.6 points per pupil at Roman Catholic schools and 35.8 points per pupil at LEA schools. This is an advantage of about 12 per cent for Church of England schools and ten per cent for Roman Catholic schools compared with LEA schools.

Pupils Leaving School With No GCSE Passes

At LEA schools, on average, 5.1 per cent of pupils leave without any GCSE passes at any grade—not even a single grade G. At Church of England and Roman Catholic schools the figure is slightly lower—around four per cent.

Sixth Forms

There are appreciable numbers of secondary schools which have no sixth forms—nearly half the total. In many areas there are sixth form colleges, or else A-level courses are available in further education colleges. In addition there may be significant numbers of pupils who leave their secondary schools at 16 and take up A-level courses elsewhere or who move from one school to another for sixth form studies. It is therefore difficult to make direct comparisons between A-level results and GCSE results. Nevertheless, it may be interesting to make some comparisons for A-level results.

Numbers of Schools with Sixth Forms (Table 7)

Church of England schools make up nearly six per cent of schools with sixth forms while Roman Catholic schools make up over 13 per cent—slightly higher proportions than for pupils from 11-16.

Table 7
Age 18 (A-level) - Secondary Schools
Percentage taking Two or More A-levels
and Points[6] per Pupil

Type of School	No. of Schools with sixth forms	% of pupils with 2 or more A-levels	Points/Pupil
LEA	1,269	32.10	15.30
Church of England	89	42.00	16.20
Roman Catholic	210	33.80	15.70

The proportion of pupils who take two or more A-levels is, on average, 42 per cent for pupils at Church of England schools compared with 33.8 per cent at Roman Catholic schools and 32.1 per cent at LEA schools.

On average, pupils at Church of England schools obtain 16.2 points which is slightly more than pupils at Roman Catholic schools—15.7 points—and LEA schools—15.3 points. This corresponds roughly to two Cs and a D if a pupil takes three subjects.

Note on Different Types of Secondary School (Tables 8-10)

The data given above for secondary schools does not distinguish between different types of school—comprehensive, secondary modern or grammar schools. Data in Tables 8-10 show GCSE results for LEA, Church of England and Roman Catholic schools of these types.

Numbers of Schools

As can be seen from Tables 8-10, most church schools are comprehensive schools and church schools make up only about ten per cent of secondary modern and grammar schools.

The most striking feature of these results is the relatively high standards reached by pupils at the widely under-rated secondary modern schools. Even for pupils achieving five or more grade A* to C at GCSE, they obtain results which are not far behind those for LEA comprehensive schools. The differences are even less for the average number of GCSE points per pupil; on this measure pupils at Roman Catholic secondary modern schools actually out-perform, on average, pupils at LEA comprehensive schools.

As expected, pupils at grammar schools of whatever kind achieve very high results.

Table 8
Age 16 (GCSE) - Comprehensive Schools

Type of School	No. of Schools	%5+A*C	Points/ Pupil	% of pupils achieving no GCSE passes A* - G
LEA	2,204	41.80	35.40	5.20
Church of England	128	50.80	39.90	4.10
Roman Catholic	322	48.50	39.40	3.80

Table 9
Age 16 (GCSE) - Secondary Modern Schools

Type of School	No. of Schools	%5+A*C	Points/ Pupil	% of pupils achieving no GCSE passes A* - G
LEA	139	30.90	30.70	5.50
Church of England	7	36.30	34.00	3.70
Roman Catholic	9	36.20	35.50	4.30

Table 10
Age 16 (GCSE) - Grammar Schools

Type of School	No. of Schools	%5+A*C	Points/ Pupil	% of pupils achieving no GCSE passes A* - G
LEA	91	95.00	58.80	0.80
Church of England	4	99.00	63.70	0.50
Roman Catholic	7	90.50	58.30	2.60

Summary

In summary, pupils at church schools, both Church of England and Roman Catholic, are, on average, ahead of pupils at LEA schools by about three months of progress at the age of seven, by about six months at the age of 11, and by between six and ten months by the age of 14.

Nevertheless pupils at church schools are achieving, on average, a little above the expectation for their age at seven but are substantially below expectations at 11 and 14—by about eight months at 11 and by about 15 months at 14.

Rates of progress for pupils at church schools are also below expectations—about three years of progress in the four years from 7 to 11 and two years of progress in the three years from 11 to 14.

Church schools perform better than LEA schools at GCSE by between ten per cent and 20 per cent, but at A-level there is very little difference, although rather more pupils take two or more A-levels.

Yet the large variations in performance of different church schools, which are described in detail in the next section, overshadow to a considerable extent their slightly better average performance compared with LEA schools.

C. Variations In Standards Between Individual Schools

The following pages show detailed distribution charts for individual LEA, Church of England and Roman Catholic schools for standards reached by pupils at the ages of seven, 11, 14, 16 and 18; in each case the vertical axis shows the number of schools.

In summary these charts show that, for nearly all the indicators, the overall performance of both Church of England and Roman Catholic schools is, on average, better than that for LEA schools—which we have already noted from the average standards discussed in Section B above. This, however, is only a part of the story. The most striking features of Figures 3-11 are the very broad distributions for each indicator and for each type of school.

At 7 years old: the average standard for all types of school —both church and LEA—is slightly above the expected national standard (vertical line) for both reading and mathematics. The spread in standards for all schools is very large—about 2.5 years—from about six to 8.5 years for both reading and mathematics.

At 11 years old: the average standard for all types of school—both church and LEA—is substantially below the expected national standard (vertical line) for both English and mathematics. The spread for LEA schools is very large —nearly 4 years—from about 8.25 to 11.75 years for both English and mathematics; the spread for church schools is a little less—about 3 years—from about nine to 12 years for both English and mathematics.

At 14 years old: the average standard for all schools is well below the expected national standard (vertical line) by about two years for both English and mathematics with mathematics slightly better than English. The spread for all schools is even larger—over six years in English and five years in mathematics. For LEA schools the range is from about eight to 14 years for English and from about 9.5 to 14.5 years for mathematics while for church schools it is from about nine to 15 years for English and from about 10 to 15 years for mathematics. There are very few schools of any kind with average subject 'ages' over 14, the actual age of the pupils.

At 16 years old: the distributions of %5A*C GCSE for all kinds of school—both church and LEA—is very broad, with the largest numbers between 20 per cent and 60 per cent but with many schools both above and below these figures. Many schools thus have five or six times fewer pupils obtaining five or more GCSE passes at Grades A* to C than other schools of the same type; more detailed analyses show that differences on this scale exist even for schools of the same type in the same or similar areas.

At 18 years old: results at A-level show variations between church schools which are just as large as for LEA schools.

It is very disturbing that, even at the age of seven, many schools of all kinds are behind the standards that they are expected to reach, particularly since the expected standard at this age is relatively undemanding.[7] By 11, more schools have fallen even further behind, and by 14, there are large numbers of church as well as LEA schools where pupils are three or more years behind in both English and mathematics.

Overall standards are poor, with the extent of underachievement increasing substantially for older pupils, and this is just as much the case for Church of England and Roman Catholic schools as it is for LEA schools.

Figure 3
Age 7 (Key Stage 1) - Primary Schools: Reading
Average Reading 'Subject Age' of 7-year-old Pupils in Individual Schools in England

LEA Schools

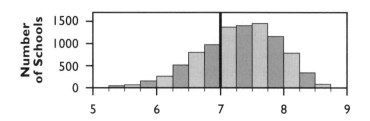

Church of England Schools

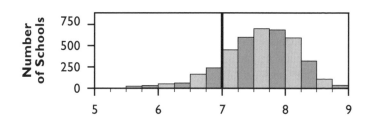

Roman Catholic Schools

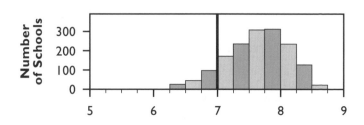

Figure 4
Age 7 (Key Stage 1) - Primary Schools: Mathematics
Average Mathematics 'Subject Age' of 7-year-old Pupils in Individual Schools in England

LEA Schools

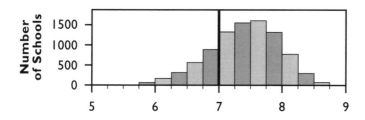

Church of England Schools

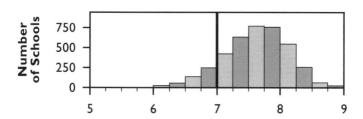

Roman Catholic Schools

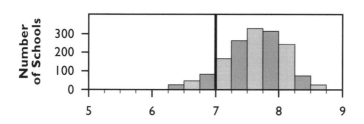

Figure 5
Age 11 (Key Stage 2) - Primary Schools: English
Average English 'Subject Age' of 11-year-old Pupils in Individual Schools in England

LEA Schools

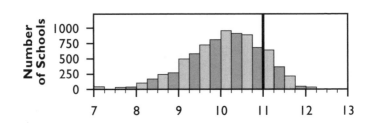

Church of England Schools

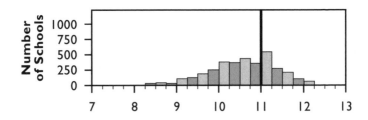

Roman Catholic Schools

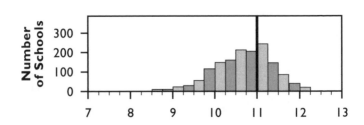

Figure 6
Age 11 (Key Stage 2) - Primary Schools: Mathematics
Average Mathematics 'Subject Age' of 11-year-old Pupils in Individual Schools in England

LEA Schools

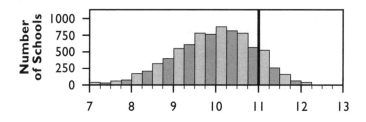

Church of England Schools

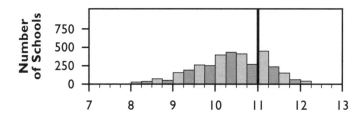

Roman Catholic Schools

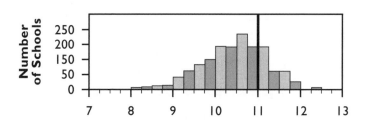

Figure 7
Age 14 (Key Stage 3) - Secondary Schools: English
Average English 'Subject Age' of 14-year-old Pupils in Individual Schools in England

LEA Schools

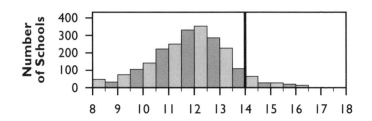

Church of England Schools

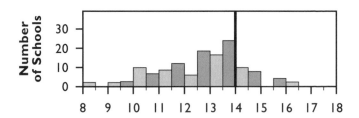

Roman Catholic Schools

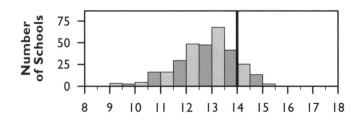

Figure 8
Age 14 (Key Stage 3) - Secondary Schools:
Mathematics

Average Mathematics 'Subject Age' of 14-year-old Pupils in Individual Schools in England

LEA Schools

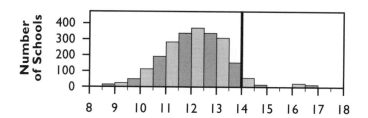

Church of England Schools

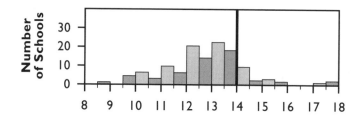

Roman Catholic Schools

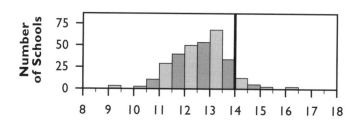

Figure 9
Current Standards in GCSE:
Percentage of Pupils Achieving Five or More GCSE
Passes at Grades A* to C in Different Types of School

LEA Schools

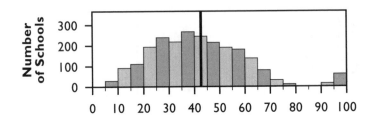

Church of England Schools

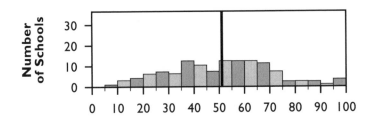

Roman Catholic Schools

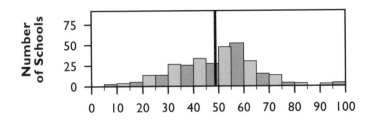

Figure 10
Current Standards in A-level:
Percentages of Pupils taking Two or More A-levels
in Different Types of School

LEA Schools

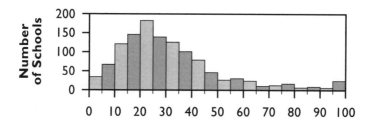

Church of England Schools

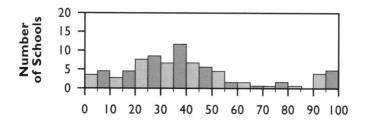

Roman Catholic Schools

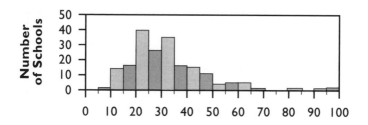

Figure 11
Mean A-level Points per Pupil
in Different Types of School

LEA Schools

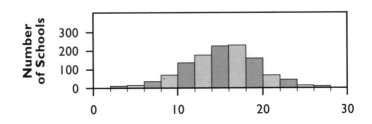

Church of England Schools

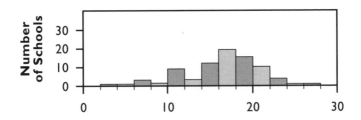

Roman Catholic Schools

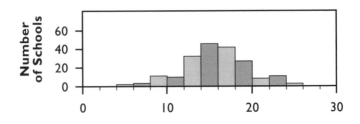

D. *Location Of Church Schools*

Tables 11 and 12 (pp. 29-36) show the percentages of primary schools and secondary schools in each LEA which are Church of England or Roman Catholic schools. It is clear that the distribution of church schools across the country is far from uniform, especially for secondary schools. For example there are only two LEAs with no Church of England primary school and two with no Roman Catholic primary school, whereas there are 71 LEAs with no Church of England secondary school and 19 with no Roman Catholic secondary school.

E. *Conclusion*

Average standards in church schools are a little higher than in LEA schools and their pupils' rates of progress are also a little higher, so that their advantage over LEA schools increases for older pupils. Nevertheless, average standards in church schools are significantly below expectations at the ages of 11 and 14.

However, this relatively favourable average performance nationally is overshadowed by the staggeringly large variations in average standards between schools. No doubt these enormous differences are due to similar reasons in church schools as the ones which operate in LEA schools.

These are likely to be:

- differential effectiveness of different teaching methods, especially in the early teaching of reading and arithmetic

- over-reliance on mixed ability grouping as opposed to setting by ability

- superior performance of selective or specialised schools compared with all-ability schools

- differential effectiveness of different philosophies of education, arguments over which have bedevilled education policy in this country for at least three decades. [8]

Therefore, in addition to encouraging the Church of England to expand the number of its schools, and its secondary schools in particular, the Dearing committee should urge the Church not to abdicate its responsibilities for standards, as it has all too often done in the recent past, in deference to the prevailing lay educational opinion. Instead the Church should investigate what is and has been happening and make its own views known on the absolutely fundamental matter of standards, which should be of major concern to all involved in the education of the next generation.

Table 11
Number and Percentage of Church of England and
Roman Catholic Primary Schools in individual LEAs

LEA Name	No. of Primary Schools	% CofE	% RC
Barking & Dagenham	34	5.88	14.70
Barnet	70	20.00	12.90
Barnsley	78	15.40	7.69
Bath & NE Somerset	56	55.40	3.57
Bexley	55	7.27	12.70
Birmingham	266	8.65	20.30
Blackburn with Darwen	51	41.20	21.60
Blackpool	28	14.30	28.60
Bolton	104	28.80	16.30
Bournemouth	22	36.40	13.60
Bracknell Forest	27	25.90	7.41
Bradford	23	0.00	17.40
Brent	48	10.40	16.70
Brighton & Hove	41	19.50	17.10
Bromley	62	12.90	12.90
Buckinghamshire	119	29.40	5.04
Bury	66	30.30	15.20
Calderdale	80	23.80	8.75
Cambridgeshire	174	33.90	1.15
Camden	37	35.10	18.90
Cheshire	261	27.20	8.81
City of Kingston upon Hull	79	5.06	8.86
City of Bristol	83	14.50	14.50
City of Derby	50	10.00	10.00
Cornwall	229	18.80	1.75
Coventry	87	8.05	21.80
Croydon	68	8.82	13.20
Cumbria	248	41.50	9.68
Darlington	26	23.10	15.40
Derbyshire	287	32.40	5.57
Devon	298	35.90	3.02
Doncaster	93	9.68	10.80
Dorset	64	57.80	7.81
Dudley	82	15.90	6.10

LEA Name	No. of Primary Schools	% CofE	% RC
Durham	208	11.50	18.30
Ealing	59	3.39	13.60
East Sussex	139	46.00	6.47
East Riding of Yorkshire	118	33.90	4.24
Enfield	55	21.80	9.09
Essex	382	29.80	6.28
Gateshead	68	1.47	25.00
Gloucestershire	225	47.10	3.56
Greenwich	62	11.30	16.10
Hackney	52	13.50	7.69
Halton	48	16.70	25.00
Hammersmith & Fulham	35	14.30	20.00
Hampshire	303	32.30	4.62
Haringey	47	17.00	17.00
Harrow	35	2.86	17.10
Hartlepool	30	13.30	20.00
Havering	48	4.17	14.60
Herefordshire	83	48.20	3.61
Hertfordshire	341	21.70	9.97
Hillingdon	49	12.20	12.20
Hounslow	45	4.44	13.30
Islington	44	20.50	15.90
Kensington & Chelsea	26	26.90	26.90
Kent	407	37.30	6.63
Kingston upon Thames	28	35.70	14.30
Kirklees	97	25.80	8.25
Knowsley	57	10.50	40.40
Lambeth	59	25.40	10.20
Lancashire	486	35.40	21.80
Leeds	224	17.00	12.90
Leicester City	68	4.41	8.82
Leicestershire	181	39.20	6.63
Lewisham	66	15.20	15.20
Lincolnshire	267	40.40	2.62
Liverpool	111	10.80	38.70
Luton	35	2.86	11.40
Manchester	125	20.80	28.80

LEA Name	No. of Primary Schools	% CofE	%RC
Medway Towns	61	8.20	13.10
Merton	12	8.33	0.00
Middlesborough	42	0.00	28.60
Milton Keynes	43	4.65	9.30
Newcastle	53	5.66	34.00
Newham	55	5.45	10.90
Norfolk	255	37.30	1.57
North Lincolnshire	56	28.60	7.14
North East Lincolnshire	40	12.50	5.00
North Tyneside	32	9.38	28.10
North Somerset	52	48.10	5.77
North Yorkshire	300	43.30	6.33
Northamptonshire	168	39.30	4.17
Nottingham City	81	3.70	9.88
Nottinghamshire	233	22.70	5.15
Oldham	85	27.10	14.10
Oxfordshire	192	52.10	5.73
Peterborough	50	22.00	4.00
Plymouth	68	10.30	8.82
Poole	15	20.00	13.30
Portsmouth	29	6.90	13.80
Reading	34	5.88	11.80
Redbridge	38	2.63	15.80
Redcar & Cleveland	46	4.35	17.40
Richmond upon Thames	32	28.10	18.80
Rochdale	76	25.00	18.40
Rotherham	82	13.40	8.54
Rutland	18	61.10	5.56
Salford	83	22.90	25.30
Sandwell	84	10.70	9.52
Sefton	85	21.20	32.90
Sheffield	118	7.63	11.00
Shropshire	131	61.80	2.29
Slough	21	9.52	19.00
Solihull	52	23.10	17.30
Somerset	164	47.60	4.88
South Gloucester	79	38.00	6.33

LEA	No. of Primary Schools	%CofE	%RC
South Tyneside	44	11.40	22.70
Southampton	38	10.50	7.89
Southend on Sea	28	3.57	14.30
Southwark	66	16.70	16.70
St Helens	55	23.60	27.30
Staffordshire	229	27.10	14.00
Stockport	87	13.80	14.90
Stockton on Tees	57	14.00	21.10
Stoke-on-Trent	74	17.60	16.20
Suffolk	111	35.10	5.41
Sunderland	84	3.57	17.90
Surrey	196	21.90	13.30
Sutton	32	12.50	9.38
Swindon	43	11.60	9.30
Tameside	77	23.40	15.60
Telford & Wrekin	50	22.00	8.00
Thurrock	37	8.11	10.80
Torbay	28	28.60	14.30
Tower Hamlets	62	14.50	14.50
Trafford	64	12.50	21.90
Wakefield	101	18.80	8.91
Walsall	74	12.20	12.20
Waltham Forest	44	6.82	9.09
Wandsworth	54	16.70	14.80
Warrington	70	25.70	21.40
Warwickshire	143	38.50	13.30
West Sussex	166	34.30	9.04
West Berkshire	58	48.30	5.17
Westminster	37	51.40	18.90
Wigan	109	35.80	27.50
Wiltshire	181	63.50	5.52
Windsor & Maidenhead	27	44.40	11.10
Wirral	92	13.00	20.70
Wokingham	39	33.30	5.13
Wolverhampton	73	19.20	13.70
Worcestershire	76	48.70	13.20
York	46	23.90	10.90

Table 12
**Number and Percentage of Church of England and
Roman Catholic Secondary Schools in individual LEAs**

LEA Name	No. of Secondary Schools	% CofE	% RC
Barking & Dagenham	8	0.00	12.5
Barnet	21	9.52	19.0
Barnsley	14	0.0	7.14
Bath & NE Somerset	13	7.69	7.69
Bedfordshire	17	5.88	5.88
Bexley	16	6.25	18.80
Birmingham	77	1.30	13.00
Blackburn with Darwen	9	11.10	22.20
Blackpool	8	0.00	12.50
Bolton	16	18.80	18.80
Bournemouth	9	0.00	11.10
Bracknell Forest	6	16.70	0.00
Bradford	23	0.00	17.40
Brent	13	0.00	23.10
Brighton & Hove	9	0.00	11.10
Bromley	17	5.88	5.88
Buckinghamshire	34	2.94	2.94
Bury	14	7.14	14.30
Calderdale	15	6.67	6.67
Cambridgeshire	29	0.00	0.00
Camden	10	0.00	20.00
Cheshire	43	2.33	11.60
City of Kingston upon Hull	15	6.67	6.67
City of Derby	14	0.00	7.14
City of Bristol	20	5.00	15.00
Cornwall	31	0.00	0.00
Coventry	19	5.26	15.80
Croydon	21	9.52	23.80
Cumbria	42	4.76	9.52
Darlington	7	0.00	14.30
Derbyshire	47	0.00	8.51
Devon	37	5.41	0.00
Doncaster	17	0.00	5.88
Dorset	20	20.00	0.00
Dudley	22	0.00	4.55
Durham	36	0.00	11.10
Ealing	13	7.69	7.69
East Sussex	25	4.00	4.00

LEA Name	No. of Secondary Schools	%CofE	%RC
East Riding of Yorkshire	18	0.00	0.00
Enfield	16	6.25	12.50
Essex	77	1.30	6.49
Gateshead	10	0.00	20.00
Gloucestershire	42	0.00	4.76
Greenwich	14	7.14	21.40
Hackney	9	11.10	22.20
Halton	9	0.00	22.20
Hammersmith & Fulham	8	25.00	25.00
Hampshire	71	0.00	2.82
Haringey	9	11.10	11.10
Harrow	10	0.00	20.00
Hartlepool	6	0.00	16.70
Havering	18	5.56	11.10
Herefordshire	14	7.14	7.14
Hertfordshire	76	6.58	9.21
Hillingdon	15	6.67	6.67
Hounslow	14	7.14	21.40
Isle of Wight	5	0.00	0.00
Isles of Scilly	1	0.00	0.00
Islington	8	0.00	25.00
Kensington & Chelsea	4	0.00	75.00
Kent	102	4.90	5.88
Kingston upon Thames	10	10.00	20.00
Kirklees	25	0.00	8.00
Knowsley	11	0.00	36.40
Lambeth	10	30.00	20.00
Lancashire	89	8.99	21.30
Leeds	43	4.65	11.60
Leicester City	15	0.00	13.30
Leicestershire	18	11.10	5.56
Lewisham	12	8.33	16.70
Lincolnshire	63	6.35	3.17
Liverpool	33	9.09	39.40
Luton	12	0.00	8.33
Manchester	20	5.00	25.00
Medway Towns	20	0.00	5.00
Merton	8	0.00	25.00
Middlesborough	11	0.00	27.30
Milton Keynes	9	0.00	11.10
Newcastle	12	0.00	25.00

LEA Name	No. of Secondary Schools	% CofE	% RC
Newham	13	0.00	15.40
Norfolk	52	1.92	1.92
North Yorkshire	42	2.38	7.14
North Lincolnshire	14	0.00	7.14
North East Lincolnshire	12	8.33	8.33
North Somerset	10	0.00	0.00
North Tyneside	11	0.00	9.09
Northamptonshire	37	2.70	5.41
Northumberland	14	0.00	7.14
Nottingham City	19	5.26	5.26
Nottinghamshire	50	6.00	6.00
Oldham	15	13.30	13.30
Oxfordshire	35	2.86	2.86
Peterborough	13	15.40	7.69
Plymouth	18	0.00	11.10
Poole	8	0.00	0.00
Portsmouth	9	11.10	11.10
Reading	8	0.00	12.50
Redbridge	15	0.00	13.30
Redcar & Cleveland	13	0.00	15.40
Richmond upon Thames	8	12.50	0.00
Rochdale	14	0.00	21.40
Rotherham	17	0.00	11.80
Rutland	3	0.00	0.00
Salford	15	6.67	26.70
Sandwell	20	5.00	5.00
Sefton	22	0.00	31.80
Sheffield	26	0.00	7.69
Shropshire	22	4.55	0.00
Slough	11	9.09	18.20
Solihull	13	0.00	15.40
Somerset	30	13.30	0.00
South Gloucester	14	0.00	0.00
South Tyneside	11	0.00	18.20
Southampton	14	0.00	14.30
Southend on Sea	12	0.00	16.70
Southwark	12	16.70	33.30
St Helens	12	0.00	33.30
Staffordshire	55	0.00	9.09
Stockport	13	0.00	15.40
Stockton on Tees	12	8.33	25.00

LEA Name	No. of Secondary Schools	%CofE	%RC
Stoke-on-Trent	17	5.88	17.60
Suffolk	38	5.26	5.26
Sunderland	17	0.00	17.60
Surrey	52	7.69	11.50
Sutton	14	7.14	14.30
Swindon	10	0.00	10.00
Tameside	18	0.00	16.70
Telford & Wrekin	13	0.00	7.69
Thurrock	10	0.00	10.00
Torbay	8	0.00	0.00
Tower Hamlets	15	13.30	13.30
Trafford	18	0.00	22.20
Wakefield	18	5.56	11.10
Walsall	20	5.00	10.00
Waltham Forest	16	0.00	6.25
Wandsworth	9	0.00	22.20
Warrington	12	0.00	16.70
Warwickshire	37	2.70	10.80
West Berkshire	9	0.00	0.00
West Sussex	36	16.70	11.10
Westminster	8	37.50	12.50
Wigan	21	9.52	23.80
Wiltshire	28	10.70	7.14
Windsor & Maidenhead	10	20.00	0.00
Wirral	23	0.00	21.70
Wokingham	9	11.10	0.00
Wolverhampton	18	11.10	11.10
Worcestershire	29	6.90	10.30
York	12	16.70	8.33

Church Schools: A Critique of Much Current Practice

John Burn

Introduction: Comments On The Church Schools Review Group Report

The Church Schools Review Group, chaired by Lord Dearing, produced its final report in June 2001.

The Church of England is concerned about the uneven provision of church schools both within dioceses and between one diocese and another. There is also an uneven provision between primary and secondary schools, with five times more pupil places in primary than in secondary schools. There is a particular concern about the complete absence of a Church of England secondary school in seven dioceses. Some important cities in urban areas—such as Sunderland, Sheffield, Newcastle upon Tyne, Plymouth and Norwich—have no maintained Church of England secondary school. The Church of England is clearly eager to create more maintained schools in partnership with local education authorities and other bodies, especially in the secondary sector.

It is startling to read in the report that the Roman Catholic church has now twice as many secondary schools as the Church of England and that, in the 50-year period since 1950, the number of Roman Catholic secondary schools has increased six-fold whilst the number of Anglican secondary schools has in fact decreased. It is also significant that whilst the Roman Catholic church has rightly pursued a policy of entirely voluntary aided schools, by contrast the Church of England has more than half of its schools in the voluntary controlled sector where the Christian emphasis is likely to be weaker.

Voluntary aided schools are better from the Church of England's point of view in that, unlike the voluntary controlled schools, Church-of-England-appointed governors predominate, and they are supported by the Department of Education and Skills by up to 85 per cent of approved expenditure. Proposals are in place to increase this to 90 per cent. In terms of staffing, the voluntary aided schools are also stronger in that the governors of the school can seek evidence of Christian commitment from applicants for teaching posts. In voluntary controlled schools governors are bound by LEA appointing policies, although governors are able to satisfy themselves that a candidate for the post of head teacher is suitable to support and develop the specified ethos of the school.

Currently the Church of England is active in exploiting opportunities to create city academies, one of whose strengths is that they are publicly funded independent schools. Of the first five such academies announced, two are to be Church of England city academies.

A Distinctively Christian Ethos

The opportunity to create more primary and secondary schools with a clear Christian ethos is to be welcomed. The issue is how distinctively Christian they will be in addressing the full development of the whole person—body, mind and spirit.

It is not enough for the Church of England to argue that their schools are distinctive because of their family atmosphere and their strong commitment to the welfare of every individual child. Most schools would claim the same and many evidence these characteristics.

Many Church of England schools are oversubscribed and popular with parents because of their commitment to good discipline and moral values and their perceived record of good academic results.

On average church schools outperform the rest of schools in the maintained sector in national curriculum tests and at GCSE. However, there is almost as wide a spread between the results of the best and the worst church schools as there is for LEA schools (see pp. 18-26).

This chapter will first describe the principles I adopted in running two successful Christian secondary schools and then suggest lessons for other Christian schools, both in establishing a lively Christian ethos and in raising academic standards. It will end with some suggestions for recruiting, training and retaining good Christian teachers.

1. Running Christian State Schools: A Personal View

It is my belief that church schools should offer a distinctively Christian-based education devoted to the promotion of the highest possible standards of behaviour and attainment for all pupils—an aim which I sought to achieve as the head of two comprehensive schools from 1979 to 1998.

Longbenton Community High School, 1979-1993

I was for 14 years—1979-93—the head of a county comprehensive school at Longbenton, in an area of North Tyneside characterised by high unemployment and low income.

When I first became head I inherited a situation which was all too familiar. There was no religious education in the curriculum of what was a large urban county comprehensive school. There was no act of worship and no Bibles existed in the school. This was in defiance of the law of the land at the time.

Gradually I was able to change the situation for the better as I attempted to create an institution of quality which took seriously the requirements of national legislation by introducing:

- a daily act of worship which was broadly and mainly Christian

- a programme of religious education which gave substantial time to Christianity

- a personal and social education programme which presented positively the Bible's teaching on sexual ethics, the family and marriage.

The introduction of a daily act of worship and of the teaching of Christianity within religious education also had

a beneficial effect on the entire ethos of the school. Aspira-
tions were raised, as was attainment.

Emmanuel College, Gateshead

From 1993 to December 1998 I was Principal of Emmanuel
College, Gateshead—a comprehensive school and a city
technology college on Tyneside. Emmanuel is not a church
school but its foundation agreement established it as a
non-denominational Christian comprehensive school
serving a predominantly inner-city area straddling the
River Tyne; two-thirds of the pupils come from areas of
disadvantage—low incomes and high unemployment.

Both Longbenton and Emmanuel were very successful
academically. Emmanuel was oversubscribed by more than
three to one and Longbenton became increasingly popular
with parents, most of whom were not church attenders or
regularly practising Christians.

How Was It Done?

Both these schools, under my headship, made it a priority
to provide young people with opportunities for them to
succeed academically and to be equipped spiritually and
morally so as to become active and concerned citizens.

The ideas which follow are based on a lifetime of experience in teaching in urban comprehensive schools and are
offered as suggestions to those with responsibility for
church and non-denominational Christian schools as they
seek to develop further in the years ahead.

The work and practice of a Christian school should be
based on and underpinned by the Christian faith. This, in
my experience, will have a huge bearing on what the school
and its pupils will achieve.

The Christian faith is realistic about human nature. It
believes that man is both fallen and redeemable. It challenges the prevailing educational orthodoxy that children
are inherently good. It takes seriously the natural inclina-
tion to evil of unregenerate man. It also believes in the
accountability of human beings ultimately to their Maker.

It offers significance, value and meaning to this present life and hope for an infinite future with God. It is a counter to the relativism and the subjectivism which are the norm in many schools and to the view that life has no ultimate meaning and significance in a universe without evidence of a Creator.

Above all, for the life of a school, the Christian faith offers divine absolutes of right and wrong as a challenge to the widely held view that 'if it feels right, do it'. The failure to present absolutes and truth in our schools is one of the prime causes of the educational ills that beset us.

An environment in which right and wrong are taught and which offers meaning and purpose to life leads young people to be positive about their own capabilities and to develop academically, morally and spiritually to the fullest extent possible.

Such a Christian environment is likely to be disciplined and to set clear limits on behaviour. It is an environment in which consistent punishment and subsequent restoration are likely to be strong and complementary features. Such an environment is safe and secure and one in which children and young people can focus on genuine learning and achievement. Teaching and learning then become everyday possibilities, rather than the 'lion taming' which is all that teachers can achieve if the school environment lacks order and structure—an all too common occurrence in many schools today.

Christian schools must also emphasise by their practice the significance, importance and value of each individual uniquely made in God's image. A close attention to the spiritual and moral development of every child will also embrace a desire to see that children fulfil to the maximum their academic potential. In striving for high academic attainment, it is important to set realistically high targets for every individual. If this is well done, then institutional targets will fall naturally into place and will exceed expectations (see below).

I would also expect Christian schools to be distinctive in other areas including:

- the daily act of worship
- the programme of religious education
- the programme of sex and personal and social education.

2. Future Directions For Church Schools

Christian Worship And Biblical Illiteracy

The Dearing Report is to be commended for recommending that every church school should engage meaningfully in Christian worship every day. Church schools should all seek to do well what national legislation requires of all schools— to ensure that at every key stage of the curriculum importance is attached to the teaching of Christianity as well as teaching the important aspects of other world faiths represented in Britain. The truth claims of the major world faiths are radically different and mutually exclusive. This situation should be respected. To ensure that the truth claims of the major faiths are properly taught is more likely to create real and genuine mutual respect and tolerance rather than bigotry and intolerance, as is often claimed.

Moreover, there is a national problem of biblical illiteracy. Church schools should seek as one of their targets the creation of a biblically literate generation.

Religious Education And Good Citizens

The report rightly stresses the need for church schools to offer good quality in religious education, but seems reluctant to spell out the importance of ensuring that the scheme of work should seek to teach the details of orthodox Christian belief and practice.

Its recommendation that religious education be given at least five per cent of school time is to be commended, as is its view that all pupils should take at least the short course GCSE and preferably the full GCSE in religious education.

It would be desirable if the law were amended to ensure a higher quality of religious education. A constructive suggestion is that all schools be given the freedom either to follow the locally agreed syllabus of any local education authority, or to create their own syllabus, and then to ask OFSTED to inspect the syllabus to ensure that it is complying with the statutory requirements as defined by the 1988 Education Reform Act.

The issue is not just the need to give sufficient time to religious education. There is also the need to give sufficient attention to content in order to counteract the baleful ignorance on the part of many of our children about the basics of Christian belief and morality.

Church schools should be beacons of excellence in the way they give proper attention to the beliefs, values and truth claims of Christianity, in particular, and also of the other major faiths represented in Britain today.

An opportunity has also been missed in the Dearing Report to argue that religious education, of all subjects in the curriculum, should be the major means by which all children learn to become good citizens.

Citizenship is, of course, about loving our neighbours as ourselves. But it is also about developing young people who appreciate the importance of personal faith and who have acquired that wisdom which comes from knowing what is true and doing what is right. Citizenship and religious education should seek to challenge positively the dangerous relativism so prevalent in society today.

Good citizenship will be promoted if schools equip young people to be confident and articulate, to have a concern for others and to know what they believe and value and why they do so.

Church Schools And Moral Issues

Church schools can help young people to see the ethical implications of the Christian faith for many issues which face us today, including abortion, euthanasia, cloning, genetic research, sexual relationships and crime and punishment.

Church schools are also well placed to offer to young people a radically different faith-based approach to personal and social education. In many church schools the personal and social education schemes are little different from that provided by their neighbouring community schools. This is a sad situation.

Christians have often described the Bible as the Maker's manual for right living which contains revealed truth and absolute 'givens' from the Creator and Lawgiver. Whilst recognising that fallen humanity fails to live by God's ideals, it is surely right that young people should encounter what God in His Word has to say about the ethical issues which confront us all.

This should clearly be done in an imaginative and sensitive way, but an education that fails to give such opportunities to young people fails them in a very real sense. The object here is certainly not to attempt to manipulate young people into belief and right living. It is to give them an opportunity of knowing the best and the highest and leaving the response to them.

One of the greatest disservices of all is to leave young people to drift in a strong current of relativism in which there are no absolutes. It is often a sign of deadness to go with the flow and a sign of real life and vitality to swim against the prevailing tide.

Sixth Forms

Many church schools have sixth forms and all such schools should ensure that the requirements in relation to the daily act of worship area are being fully met.

I would expect to see a significant amount of time being given to a broad programme of religious education to all sixth form students in every church school. This would contribute enormously to their spiritual, moral and intellectual development and would play a major part in the further development of their ability to think and argue.

Within this programme, sixth formers would be able to think through in a deep way and with rigour the major issues which face them and us. They should be looked at from the standpoint of a variety of world-views including atheism, naturalism, Islam, scientism, humanism, Eastern world-views and Christianity.

Such a course would make an excellent contribution to education for citizenship, parenthood and the world of work. More importantly it would help maturing young persons to acquire for themselves a coherent, meaningful and satisfying personal faith and moral code.

Sex And Relationships Education

The Dearing Report is, however, disappointing in not giving any clear guidance about sex and relationships education. The opportunity to commend positively the biblical view—sexual abstinence outside of marriage and fidelity within it—has not been taken, This is one area surely where church schools could and should be conspicuously different.

There is much contemporary concern about the high rate of teenage pregnancy, and the received wisdom seems to be that the teaching of safe sex has been largely abandoned in schools. The question is whether it should have begun in the first place. There is now to be strong pressure on schools from the health authorities for them to dispense the 'morning after' pill to secondary pupils. It is to be hoped that church schools, through their head teachers and boards of governors, will strongly resist this.

Many would argue that the problem is not lack of information but lack of attention to the moral development of young people in schools.

Church schools, reflecting the biblical basis of the Christian faith, have a significant opportunity positively to present sexual abstinence and sex within marriage alone, and so challenge the 'value free' relativism of much sex and relationships education.

The report does, in fairness, state that the Church offers a spiritual and moral basis for the development of human wholeness and a sure foundation for personal and social values based on the person and ministry of Christ. This is, of course, true, and that sure basis is spelt out in the whole of scripture.

This moral basis needs articulating and grounding in the personal and social education curriculum of church schools. It is a basis shared to a considerable extent by the major monotheistic religions.

As this chapter was being written, I was contacted by a Church of England minister and a member of the governing body of a Church of England controlled primary school which was in the process of revising its programme of sex education. The minister concerned had been advised, by his diocesan education adviser, against arguing for marriage as being a better option than loving and stable relationships in the wording of that church school's sex education policy.

The adviser was at pains to say that his was of course a personal viewpoint. Nevertheless, the dialogue reveals the confusion within the church itself and the lack of desire to be distinctively Christian. This kind of situation is far more commonplace than is admitted in public.

3. Raising Expectations And Academic Standards

As we have seen, the biblical view of human nature and human potential is such that it produces an environment of safety and success. Expectations by pupils, staff and parents rise. An awareness of the moral rightness of punishment for transgression and the living enactment by teachers of subsequent forgiveness and restoration produces an environment in which pupils can grow spiritually and morally, and thus also raise their educational attainment.

It is, of course, true that in general church schools do well in public examinations, such as national curriculum tests and GCSE, although performance is not uniformly good even taking into account the social and economic realities of the neighbourhood. Even schools with a respectable-looking position in the performance tables may be coasting rather than stretching all of their pupils.

In my experience, if the focus is on the spiritual, moral, physical, mental and academic development of each individual child in the school, then examination targets can almost take care of themselves.

Church schools which are distinctively Christian in what they seek to do could even more readily become beacons of excellence and exemplars of true holistic education. Parents and pupils alike expect schools to help every single child gain the highest possible qualifications to equip them for their future. Such an ambition for all children is not the enemy of spiritual and moral growth, rather is it the fruit of personal spiritual and moral growth.

To achieve this, however, we must not despise systems and rigour and routines such as benchmarking and target-setting. As children develop from the early years, through primary education and into secondary education, there should be an increasing emphasis on giving them meaning-ful educational targets. The organisation must also be in place to help children meet and if possible exceed those targets.

I am not here suggesting an arid and mechanistic approach to children's learning. There is, however, a place for objectivity, precision and the setting of realistic targets in the interest of the development of all children, especially for children who find learning difficult or who lack support at home.

Children, and their parents, need to be given an honest appraisal of where they are and the steps and measures they need to take to help them to succeed. It is neither loving nor caring to mislead or fail to inform.

As far as resources and timetabling allow, children should be placed in sets by attainment, in all subjects and in every year of secondary school. This is important for all children, not least those with the most learning difficulties. There is also a great deal to be said for giving benchmarks and targets throughout the school which have some correla-tion with the grades awarded at GCSE from A* to G.

Children and their parents must be given this informa-tion. A regular system of reporting to parents should indicate what the targets are and the practical steps which children will be expected to take, with the support and encouragement of their parents and their teachers, in order for these targets to be met. This must, of course, be handled sensitively and in a positive manner with an in-built expectation of success.

Experience at Emmanuel College, Gateshead, demon-strates clearly that this system produces outstanding success in terms of academic achievement, with quite striking proof of massive success from many children who start their secondary years with low attainment and low IQ (see Table 1). Such a system could play a huge part in raising attainment nationally in a quite significant way. But, in my experience, the surrounding ethos is another crucial factor.

Table 1
Emmanuel College GCSE Results, 1995 - 2000

Year	%5A*C		%A*C English		%A*C Maths	
	EC	NA	EC	NA	EC	NA
1995	75.2	41.6	78.7	56.9	60.3	44.7
1996	79.0	42.6	88.7	56.8	67.6	46.5
1997	90.3	43.3	99.5	56.0	85.2	47.3
1998	88.0	44.6	92.2	56.5	82.0	46.9
1999	90.0	46.6	97.7	57.7	89.3	48.1
2000	98.0	47.4	98.4	57.8	84.9	47.8

Key: EC: Emmanuel College; NA: National Average
%5A*C: Percentage of the age group gaining five or more GCSE passes at grades A* to C
%A*C: Percentage of the age group gaining A* to C for English language or mathematics.

The national average for %5A*C (the percentage of the age group gaining five or more GCSE passes at grades A* to C) has risen slowly from 1995 to 2000, from about 42 per cent to 47 per cent.

For Emmanuel College, %5A*C started at nearly twice the national average, has risen more rapidly than the national average—by 23 percentage points compared with six percentage points—and is now at the staggeringly high figure of 98 per cent.

The national average for %A*C English (the percentage of the age group gaining GCSE passes at grades A* to C in English language) has risen very slowly from 1995 to 2000, from about 57 per cent to 58 per cent.

For Emmanuel College, %A*C English started at over 20 percentage points above the national average, has risen much more rapidly than the national average—by 20 percentage points compared with one percentage point—and is now at the staggeringly high figure of 98.4 per cent.

The national average for %A*C mathematics (the percentage of the age group gaining GCSE passes at grades A* to C in mathematics) has risen very slowly from 1995 to 2000, from about 45 per cent to 48 per cent.

For Emmanuel College, %A*C mathematics started about 15 percentage points above the national average, has risen much more rapidly than the national average—by 25 percentage points compared with three percentage points—and is now at the very high figure of 85 per cent.

4. Recruiting, Training and Retaining Christian Teachers

All schools—church, non-denominational and all others—are finding it very difficult to recruit good staff. There is a critical shortage of good teachers and a great need for more Christian teachers. The issue is not simply or necessarily mainly one of pay. It also includes conditions in schools.

Church schools, Christian and other faith schools, are more likely to be places of security for children insofar as they are normally committed to sound and firm discipline. They are also likely to be more appealing for teachers for this reason. Teachers want to be able to get on with their main business of teaching without distraction and interruption.

The report is to be commended for its recommendation that, through all dioceses, parishes could be repeatedly urged to put before people what it means to be a Christian teacher and encourage the sense of vocation to teach. The success of educational reforms depends in large measure on a good supply of morally wholesome men and women with the ability and desire to achieve the very best for all children. There is also a need for head teachers of church schools to create an environment in which academic excellence for all pupils is pursued in a Christian context.

Although there has been some improvement in the training of teachers, the situation remains unsatisfactory. It is clear that good church schools, Christian schools and other faith schools, will need to have a higher profile in the whole area of initial teacher training and continuing in-service training.

There is much scope for such schools to be involved in school-centred training and taking on responsibility for ensuring that the teachers of the future are trained in centres of excellence which are infused by a distinct Christian or other faith ethos. Such schools should also see themselves taking on programmes of in-service training for teachers currently in service.

Conclusion: A Lesson From History For The Twenty-First Century

The roots of the current confusion go back to the nineteenth century. The 1870 Education Act had aimed to build on the existing settlement of mainly voluntary schools by completing the voluntary system and filling up the gaps in provision.

The intentions were honourable. The relationship over the years, however, suggests that the partnership with local authorities has in many instances weakened the position of Christianity in many Church of England schools. Too often, the Church of England schools have been insufficiently distinctively Christian. The Dearing Report of 2001 rightly seeks to reverse this unhappy trend.

It is difficult now to disagree with Lord Shaftesbury who, at the time of the passage onto the statute book of the 1870 Education Act, was more clear than most of his contemporaries that the Act would lead to the secularisation of schools. Shaftesbury was convinced that the state system of schooling would become more powerful than the voluntary and church schools, and that we would see less and less vital Christianity in schools. He has been proved right.[1]

The challenge for the churches and for all Christians now is to regain that Christian ethos in our church schools in the very different situation of the twenty-first century.

The Church in Education

Peter Pilkington

Since the conversion of Constantine, which transformed the Christian church from a persecuted sect to an integral part of society, the church has been involved in education. Godliness and good learning were seen as an essential part of the educational process, and David Newsome began his book *Godliness and Good Learning* with the following dialogue:

> 'What is a college without a chapel?' Bishop Christopher Wordsworth once asked a friend who was a Canon of Winchester Cathedral. 'An angel without wings' was the reply.[1]

The nineteenth century saw a great expansion of educational provision, and the churches, especially the Church of England, took a leading part in this process.

At this time the Church of England largely opposed state involvement in education. In the 1850s Archdeacon Dennison had said:

> So long as the civil power would help the spiritual power to do God's work in the world in these terms of which alone the spiritual power could be the fitting judge ... it ought to be thankfully received... The school of the English parish is the nursery of Catholic faith and apostolic discipline.

Another priest, the Reverend W. Sewell, said simply and directly:

> The state shall not without a creed, without a sacrament and without any ministerial authority from God, undertake to educate the people of this country.

Church of England schools were denominational and were expected to teach the doctrines of the established Church. Similarly, Catholic and non-conformist schools were in the same position with respect to their own faiths.

There were liberal clergy who opposed this rigidity, and for several years the annual meetings of the National Society were the scenes of pitched battles between liberals and high churchmen. Liberals accused the high churchmen of preferring to keep children in ignorance rather than let them receive light not tinted by themselves—a division of opinion that continues to this day.

The 1870 Education Act established a state education system, though the denominational schools (mainly Anglican) were left untouched. In the new state schools religious instruction should 'exclude any catechism or religious formulary distinctive of any particular denomination'. However, the English state schools, unlike those of France and the USA, still allowed religious instruction, though of a non-confessional style.

Most Anglican clergy disliked the 1870 Act and the practice of the church from 1870 to the start of the Second World War was to fight hard for the continuance of denominational schools. There were often bitter battles between non-conformists and Anglicans, particularly around 1914 when Welsh dis-establishment aroused sectarian passion. Yet, up to 1939, although many deplored these denominational battles, the idea of schools tied to the church was still attractive to many Anglicans. Church training colleges felt they existed to send committed Anglicans into church schools. Almost all colleges expected their students to be regular communicants, and chapel was often compulsory. When I was a curate in Derbyshire in the early 1960s, the church schools had very close connections with the parish church and every effort was made to appoint head teachers and other staff who were practising Anglicans.

The 1944 Education Act ushered in the era of voluntary aided schools and agreed syllabuses. In aided schools the church provided 15 per cent of the cost of new building and foundation and church-appointed governors controlled the governing body. The teachers were paid by the local authority, which also provided equipment and maintenance. The governors of such a school would have the right to appoint staff, control the use of the building for non-school purposes, decide the pattern of religious instruction and, subject to national educational policy, arrange the curriculum and determine admissions policy. Thus an aided school is in effect controlled by the church and could see its role as designing a pattern of education within the framework of church teaching. The voluntary controlled school (created by the 1944 Act) would be maintained wholly by the local authority and the church would have no responsibility for buildings, though they would remain the property of the governing body. Only one third of the governing body would be appointed by the church and religious instruction would be on the same agreed syllabus as that followed in local authority schools.

At present there are 774,000 pupils in Anglican primary schools and 150,000 in secondary schools, compared to 411,000 pupils in Roman Catholic primary schools and 309,000 in secondary schools. However, many of the Anglican schools are voluntary controlled, while *all* the Roman Catholic schools are aided.[2]

These figures show that the Anglican and Roman Catholic churches have since 1944 followed different policies with regard to education. The Church of England has not felt that denominational education should be maintained at all costs and has allowed, even encouraged, many schools to become voluntary controlled. In contrast the Roman Catholic church has vigorously supported its denominational schools and maintained a strong position in secondary education. There are only 150 Anglican secondary schools as compared to 580 Catholic secondary schools.

In the 1960s, many in the Church felt guilty about denominational schools and the Durham Report of 1970, though it in the end supported the maintenance of the dual system (albeit with a reduced role for the church), seemed to have some doubts about many aspects of the church schools. Certainly it was not a document which saw Anglican schools in the same light as the Roman Catholic church saw its schools. The Catholic church expended large resources on its educational provision and meant them to be bastions of Catholic faith largely staffed by Catholic teachers. This was not the situation in many Anglican schools, and the 1960s and 1970s witnessed the secularisation of many of the former church training colleges, which in many cases became indistinguishable from their secular counter-parts. The Church of England seemed to see its role (in church schools) as being the leaven in the lump rather than the city set on the hill. A paper published by the National Society in 1984 set out the ideals of a church school, either aided or voluntary controlled. The talk is of the school being a safe place where there is no ideological pressure, an ecumenical nursery creating a sensitivity to other faiths, a place of distinctive excellence extending further than the narrowly academic. The authors feel no guilt at the sharing of common ground with secular humanism, nor do they seem anxious that this might not represent the ideals of Christians working in state schools. They write:

> if ... practice corresponds closely to the practices of secular colleagues, the Christian teacher must be profoundly grateful that he is able to share common ground and he will resist the temptation to claim for his own practice a Christian distinctiveness in which his secular colleagues cannot share.[3]

There is much that is admirable in these views but they are totally different from the thinking of the Catholic church in relation to its schools.

In December 2000 a consultation report prepared by Sir Ron Dearing was circulated. In this report Sir Ron and his colleagues argued for an expansion of Church of England schools in areas where there are few and also a great increase in the number of secondary schools. They argued further that these schools should have a definite Christian ethos. They believed there should be a close relationship with the parish church and suggested that governors should ensure that the school is led by a head teacher who is committed with the help of his staff to maintaining the Christian character of the school. They also wanted meaningful Christian worship every day and the observance of major Christian festivals. Though they showed sensitivity to ecumenical issues and the place of other faiths, they recommended that church schools must be distinctively places where the Christian faith is alive and proclaimed. Naturally, in view of this policy, many Christian teachers must be recruited.

Thus Dearing and his colleagues followed a line of thinking which is much more positive than that suggested in the Durham Report or the National Society paper. In view of the increasing secularisation of society, the Dearing Report deserves our support, in that it is attempting to create a strong and active Christian presence in education.

However, it is crucial that the problems created by this approach are faced squarely. The Dearing Report says that the development of Christian schools:

> will bear directly on the ability of church schools to recruit the Christian teachers they need to give them their distinctive character.[4]

It is this long-term issue, more than any other, upon which the future of church schools depends. This will mean the church training colleges taking a more direct role in producing Christian teachers than they have in the past. It remains questionable whether some of them would be prepared to be so pro-active, since many of their staff are not practising Christians.

The other major problem will be that of finance. The Dearing Report recognises the substantial advantage in aided status, but states that if it is to be extended it would mean more financial input from the Church or other sources.

The Church of England at present faces financial difficulties, and it is hard to see it finding resources to increase greatly its secondary schools. Alternative sources of funding would have to be found. The government experienced great difficulty in finding private donors for the city technology colleges, and local authorities might not be prepared to give money for the creation of church secondary schools. The Roman Catholic church has made great sacrifices to maintain its schools but it is doubtful if there would be a consensus in the Church of England for a similar sacrifice.

A further question left unanswered in the Dearing Report is what form the new church schools will take. In the past the Church has accepted without question the state's educational policy. However, the educational world is changing and the government is talking of specialist schools. It might be desirable that the Church should take a lead in these matters. Thus, its schools might not only be bastions of faith but also satisfy the needs of particular areas. For example, certain inner city schools could develop as vocational and technical centres. There might also be a case for building up centres of academic excellence in poor areas so that educational progress was not decided by postal code.

In general, the Dearing Report is to be welcomed. It makes a return to a more robust defence of church schools which was largely abandoned in the 1960s and 1970s. However, there is much ground to be recovered and many questions remain unanswered.

How the Will of Parliament on Religious Education was Diluted by Civil Servants and the Religious Education Profession

Penny Thompson

But you can teach Christianity as true. It was the considered and widely held view, understood and accepted by both believers and unbelievers, that the provisions [of the 1988 Education Reform Act] allowed for, and were intended to create, a situation where Christianity could be taught in the classroom as true.

Graham Leonard, former Bishop of London

So read the notes of my interview, on 16 November 1998, with Fr Graham Leonard, former Chairman of the Church of England Board of Education and spokesman for the Church of England in the House of Lords when the 1988 Education Reform Act was passed. I could hardly believe my ears. I had taught religious education from 1988 to 1998 and I had never heard anyone say that Christianity could be taught as true. Indeed I had been led to believe the opposite: that the law prohibited teaching anything as true. So began my search for what the law says about religious education.

Hansard shows what those passing the law had intended. Kenneth Baker, Secretary of State for Education, believed that religious education should open up the spiritual dimension and that it was difficult for an agnostic or atheist to 'instruct children in religious education as an atheist does not believe in any kind of theistic philosophy'. So the Secretary of State believed that religious education was instruction in some kind of theism.

In fact Kenneth Baker, like Graham Leonard, believed that the teaching given would normally, but not always, be based on Christianity. This was indicated by section 8 (3) of the Act:

> ... an agreed syllabus shall reflect the fact that the religious traditions of Great Britain are in the main Christian, whilst taking account of the teachings and practices of the other principal religious traditions in Great Britain.

This was explained by the Bishop of London in the Lords:

> It does not mean that there will be a percentage of Christian teaching spread throughout the country with a proportion of other faiths ... The norm will be Christian if one likes to put it that way. But there will be exceptions because of local areas and what is proper to them in the educational setting. That is what we mean by 'mainly'—not 'mainly' in the sense of two-thirds rice and one-third tapioca or something like that.[1]

When pressed in the House on what this meant he replied:

> It is the purpose of that package [the amendments now in law] that Christian children should receive teaching in the Christian faith. Secondly, it is the purpose that children of other faiths should be taught their own faiths.[2]

Further on in the debate the Bishop put it like this:

> ... if one looks at the country as a whole, one will see that there will be areas in which it is 100 per cent [Christian traditions] and areas in which it will be less and so on.[3]

This was backed up in other parts of the legislation. The syllabus conferences which write the religious education syllabuses were to be made up of representatives from religions present in the area and in proportion to their numbers. Where there were no Muslims (or Methodists for that matter) in an area, there could be no representation on the syllabus conference. To give maximum flexibility, explicit provision was made[4] for a conference to agree more than one syllabus. No co-options could be made onto the conference,[5] although non-conference representatives could be consulted or serve as members of advisory working parties. All this meant was that only those living in the area were to determine what was to be taught.

The provisions for compulsory religious worship go to great lengths to provide for worship that is appropriate for the children receiving it. This fits in with the syllabus conference being structured to provide a religious education tailored to the pupils receiving it, which itself is the main reason for having local determination of religious education. As Kenneth Baker said:

> Nor would we presume to require that religious education should be the same in county schools in Devon as in schools in Bradford.[6]

Some peers recognised that the wording of section 8 (3) was potentially ambiguous and might not prove sufficiently strong to withstand the sort of religious education about which many had misgivings—a way of teaching which did not teach a religion for its own sake but rather relied on the use of themes such as worship, founders and festivals. This approach did not give a real grounding in any one particular religion and was dubbed a 'mishmash'.

Several amendments were tabled which offered less ambiguous wording but these were withdrawn on the understanding that they were unnecessary since both Baroness Hooper for the Government and the Bishop of London, supported by Lord Elton, insisted that their proposals:

- meant an end to mishmash

- would require Christian education for Christian children

- would give proper rights to parents of non-Christian children.

On this basis the law went to the Commons where an attempt was made by Jack Straw—then the opposition frontbench spokesman on education—to require the Secretary of State to bring in the new requirements education authority by education authority, rather than require them all to change at once. This was because he did not like the law as it stood and was concerned that teachers did not want it either. It would seem that he expected the Government to insist on the meaning given in parliament and was trying to mitigate its effects. His amendment was rejected and the law was passed intact.

The press reported the outcome accurately. For example, the *Independent* reported that:

the package of measures proposed a new basis for religious education in schools, expressing the centrality of Christianity but acknowledging and providing for the valid concerns of other religions. Agreed syllabuses should in the main be Christian but there was room for flexibility in areas where the vast majority of pupils were from another faith. So a school predominantly Muslim could draw on the traditions of that faith.[7]

Initially, some within the profession were extremely worried about the new law. John Hull wrote an editorial in the *British Journal of Religious Education* (BJRE) in July 1988 just as the clauses were going through parliament. He reacted angrily, speaking of the:

imposition of Christian supremacy through legislation.

The 'Christianising amendments' threatened to undo all the good that had been accruing in the last 20 or 25 years, in particular the:

unique British experience of multi-faith dialogue in the classroom.[8]

Some members of the Religious Education Council (REC)[9] disliked the Act intensely and had contacted Jack Straw with their concerns. But the law was passed in the Commons on 18 July.

DES Guidance On The Act

Circular 3/89

In late September, the Department of Education and Science (DES) issued a draft circular explaining the new requirements on religious education and collective worship. The circular is a model of clarity and prescription, setting out both the essential continuity with the 1944 Education Act and what had changed—in particular, that now that religious education was part of the 'basic curriculum', its importance was enhanced.

The circular set out four specific changes in relation to agreed syllabuses. The first was the requirement of section 8 (3) set out without comment:

all new syllabuses must 'reflect the fact that the religious traditions in Great Britain are in the main Christian whilst taking account of the teachings and practices of the principal religions represented in Great Britain'.[10]

The second was that, while study of denominational formularies and catechisms was now allowed, 'teaching by means of' such statements[11] continued to be prohibited.

The third laid upon the LEA the duty of giving effect to a new syllabus only if:

it appears to the authority to comply with the requirement of section 8 (3) as to the nature of religious education.[12]

The fourth amended the wording concerning the composition of syllabus conferences to make it clear that representatives of non-Christian religions could be appointed in accordance with their presence in an area.

It is striking that the circular refrained entirely from any attempt to explain section 8 (3) while requiring the LEA to decide whether a syllabus presented to them was in conformity with it. Nowhere in the whole of a lengthy circular is there any explanation of this clause. Yet it had been clearly explained by its promoters in parliament, and Jack Straw had been sufficiently concerned about it to attempt to delay the implementation of the new Act. The circular did not avoid explaining a parallel phrase concerning the legal requirements for collective worship which states that the collective worship organised by a county school was to be 'wholly or mainly of a broadly Christian character':

In the Secretary of State's view, an act of worship which is 'broadly Christian' need not contain only Christian material provided that, taken as a whole, it reflects the traditions of Christian belief ... It is not necessary for every act of worship to be of this character, but within each school term, the majority of acts of worship must be so.[13]

The circular went on to state that decisions about collective worship were to be made after considering the family backgrounds of pupils, in particular the faith of the families and the ages and aptitudes of pupils. Moreover, the circular gave full explanations of many other matters including:

- determinations[14]
- the right of withdrawal

- the provision of denominational religious education for withdrawn children
- the rights of teachers
- information and complaints.

And yet no-one could accuse the Department of neglecting to stress the importance of section 8 (3). Of all the legal provisions to do with religious education, this clause alone was considered sufficiently weighty to require a local education authority to reject the work of a syllabus conference in its entirety if, in their opinion, it was contravened. Any syllabus which did not reflect the fact that the religious traditions of the country were in the main Christian, whilst taking account of the teachings and practices of the other principal religions, was to be rejected, no matter how much time, effort and money had been spent on it and no matter how accurately in other respects the syllabus complied with the law. But the weight thus given to the clause was reduced effectively to zero by the refusal to explain what parliament intended it to mean. The clause was in effect neutered but in such a way that no-one could accuse the Department of neglecting it.

Why did the Department fail to give guidance on section 8 (3)? I have been unable to get replies to this question. The minutes of the executive committee of the Religious Education Council (REC) of a meeting in September 1988 report that a decision had been taken by the DES not to interpret the Act but to leave it to the courts. But the whole point of a circular is to explain an Act of Parliament.

The DES Refusal To Answer Queries

Understandably, religious education advisers and agreed syllabus conferences sought advice from the DES on the meaning of section 8 (3). In the minutes of the REC executive meeting held on 19 September 1988 an officer of the Inner London Education Authority (ILEA) stated:

> ILEA had been unable to obtain answers from the DES on a variety of fundamental questions.

The religious education adviser for Newcastle upon Tyne authority contacted the DES for help on issues such as what percentage of time should be given to Christianity in view of the requirement to:

> reflect the fact that the religious traditions were in the main Christian.

He found the DES reluctant to give guidance and commented that other LEAs had had similar experiences. As a result LEAs 'were not seeing things too clearly'.[15] This is borne out by the results of a research project published in May 1989 which documented confusion and uncertainty in LEA advisers' understanding of the Act. They felt that while there could be many interpretations of 'in the main Christian', some form of emphasis on Christian faith was required. In relation to 'taking account of ...' there was a division of opinion between those who thought this meant that attention to other religions was to be secondary to reflecting the Christian traditions and those who understood that now the teaching of other faiths was to be accorded equal time and attention as the teaching of Christianity.

Overall one can see the advisers struggling to make sense of the new requirements with such phrases as 'means for me', 'indicates hopefully' or 'must mean' (in the sense of this seems right).

Interestingly, one of the few areas of certainty amongst some advisers was the need to recognise the religions practised in their area.[16] These advisers were certain that syllabuses would differ from area to area because of the need to take account of local religions. Presumably they were remembering the debates in parliament. But with the DES refusing to give authoritative guidance, exactly what the law required became an open question.

Interpretations Given By The Religious Education Profession

This apparent policy of allowing the interpretation of section 8 (3) to go into free-fall presented those within the profession who disliked it with an opportunity to create and promote an alternative interpretation. By November 1988, John Hull had written *The Act Unpacked*—a word for word exegesis of section 8 (3) which ignored the careful explanations given less than six months earlier in parliament.

Hull's exegesis stated that 'in the main' meant mainly and referred to a percentage of time to be given to the Christian traditions (the tapioca and rice mixture specifically stated to be incorrect—see p. 58) and that 'taking account of' meant that the other principal religions must be taught in every syllabus. So Hull could write:

> for the first time, therefore, the basic curriculum of children and young people in our schools will not be meeting the legal standards unless they are taught the teaching of the principal non-Christian religions in Great Britain.[17]

This meaning was never raised in either House and ran counter to the main thrust of all the debates. Parliament intended to legislate for proper religious education to be given to those of other faiths alongside those being taught by means of the Christian traditions. Clearly a small section on a syllabus which majored on Christianity could never deliver that.

Hull's new interpretation was seized on enthusiastically by others. In November 1988 we read:

> while the syllabus may reflect the important place of Christianity in Great Britain, it should also recognise the important presence of other faiths. It will not be sufficient to engage in a study of Islam in Bradford and not in Truro, for the wording of the Act refers to 'Great Britain'.[18]

Kenneth Baker had intended something quite different.

In the Spring 1989 editorial of the *BJRE* Hull went further and suggested names and numbers of the principal religions now presumed to be required by law:

> the new Act requires the local Agreed Syllabus to take account not so much of the religious traditions present in the locality but those represented in Great Britain. On any reckoning, Judaism, Islam, Hinduism, the Sikh faith and Buddhism are major religious traditions which are represented in Great Britain ... no Agreed Syllabus will meet the requirements of this section of the Act unless it takes account of their teaching and practice.[19]

Hull ignored other aspects of the legislation which restricted the syllabus conference to representation from religious communities present in an area. This provision is a major problem for Hull's interpretation since, if the law required the principal religions to be taught, it would surely have provided for the conference to have experts or adherents appointed as members.

However, this was not a problem for the Religious Education Council, which produced a handbook to help Standing Advisory Committees on Religious Education (SACREs) and syllabus conferences in their work which effectively misrepresented this aspect of the law. This handbook follows Hull's interpretation of section 8 (3) and says that in light of the requirement to look beyond the local community:

> it is important that all these aspects of the context of religious education are reflected, as far as possible, in the composition of the Agreed Syllabus Conference. The first committee must include representatives of 'non-Anglican' Christian churches (Roman Catholic, as well as major Free Church traditions) as well as people from the other principal religious traditions.[20]

Yet the law specifically prohibits the appointment of representatives of religions or denominations of religions which are not present in an area.

While all this was going on the DES remained silent. Civil servants did nothing to correct these interpretations which clearly contradicted the law as explained in parliament.

Other Interpretations

In the meantime other interpretations were forthcoming. In 1989 Edwin Cox and Josephine Cairns, colleagues at the London Institute of Education, published their account of the Act.[21] They regretted the fact that conferences were unable to appoint members of religions not present in the area and said nothing about all religions now being required to be taught.[22] The Act, they argued, viewed the purpose of religious education as initiation into a religious tradition, generally Christianity. The retention of the conscience clauses underlined this and may have suggested that it was expected that teachers would teach on the basis of their own understanding and possession of faith.

The same period saw articles from two lawyers. A. Bradney of Leicester University believed that the Act strengthened Christian teaching and worship in schools, now protected by statute. The law had 'ostentatiously abandoned any idea of neutrality in matters of religion'.[23] However he warned that implementation might not be forthcoming: some unions had expressed disquiet along with some teachers. J.D.C. Harte, a barrister and academic at Newcastle University, interpreted the law along similar lines. He wrote of criticism being 'partly a reflex reaction against new law which contradicts prevailing orthodoxy in school religious education'.[24] He made a telling point when he wrote of those within the profession who had 'devised pluralist or sociological approaches to religion which they feel are threatened'.[25] Like Bradney, he wondered whether the opportunity to reassert the Christian heritage in the life and teaching of the schools would be taken.

The original meaning expressed in parliament was set out in a pamphlet published by the Campaign for Real Education (CRE) in 1990.[26] It stated that the 1988 Act was intended to reinforce the role of schools in giving children the opportunity to grow up within a religious faith and tradition, which is usually Christian in this country. However, the pamphlet stressed that the Act gave full freedom to parents of other faiths to have their children worship and be educated in conformity with their own religious and philosophical convictions. But, within the religious education profession, Hull's interpretation was gaining ground steadily and new syllabus conferences continued to produce syllabuses of a 'mishmash' character.

Defending The New Interpretation

These interpretations served to stir memories of the parliamentary debates, and questions continued to be asked about why it was that it seemed as if nothing had changed in RE. It was therefore necessary for those within the religious education profession who disliked the law to defend their interpretation. The National Society,[27] a Church of England and Church in Wales education service, had played a pivotal role in the drafting of the amendments and indeed in negotiating with Kenneth Baker and the DES in the period leading up to and during the passing of the ERA. In 1989 a booklet[28] was published purporting to answer queries and misunderstandings about the new Act, putting an authoritative case for what the law really said.

It said the law was changed to highlight the important place of religious education in the education system of the country but omitted to mention the concerns felt about a dilution of Christian teaching and mishmash.

It said, correctly, that schools did not have to approach pupils as committed Christian believers but omitted to mention the right of non-Christian pupils to have religious education in their own faith, and therefore not to be taught largely by means of the Christian traditions.

The answer to the question whether all pupils in a school should receive the same programme of religious education was a firm 'yes' despite the fact that the law clearly allows for more than one syllabus to be employed in a school.[29] The booklet argued that parents should not need to make use of withdrawal and might even be found to be intolerant in so doing. It acknowledged however that provision had to be made for those parents who 'persist in withdrawing'.

A section of the law was quoted out of context and implied that the law expected head teachers to establish with a parent requesting withdrawal an understanding of the religious issues the parent objected to. This was quite wrong. The section from the circular quoted by the booklet referred to the situation in those primary schools where religious education was integrated within other subjects and not to withdrawal *per se*.

Following John Hull, the booklet stated:

in every school all pupils ... will be expected to acquire some knowledge of Christianity and some knowledge of 'the other principal religions', i.e. Judaism, Islam, Hinduism, Sikhism and possibly Buddhism.

Articles were written by many professionals between 1988 and 1991 to support the interpretation favoured by John Hull and the National Society.[30] But soon it became unnecessary for them to insist on their view, since it was endorsed by the DES.

The DES Gives A View Following The Ealing Case

In March 1991 the DES finally gave a view on the interpretation of section 8 (3) when a letter was sent to all chief education officers to clarify the law. A year later, further advice on the nature of religious education was given in a document called *Starting Out with the National Curriculum*. The Department had been involved with a parent in Ealing who had complained that the syllabus did not comply with the requirement to 'reflect the fact that the religious traditions of Great Britain are in the main Christian'. The Department took legal advice which was relayed to all chief education officers. The Department followed counsel's opinion in its entirety. It took the view that a syllabus must give sufficient particulars for it to be clear that the teaching given would comply with the provision. In most cases most attention would be given to the Christian traditions. However, a syllabus must not be based on Christianity alone, or 'exclude from its teaching any of the principal religions represented in Great Britain'. In addition, the Department, using the exact words of counsel, stated that a syllabus 'must not be designed to convert pupils, or to urge a particular religion or religious belief on pupils'.

Counsel had assumed *The Act Unpacked* to be 'factually accurate'[31] and the influence of John Hull is clear to see. The barrister asked within the RE profession as to the standing of John Hull. He was told that there was 'none better'.[32] On the basis of this recommendation he accepted at face value all that *The Act Unpacked* argued. This was to have weighty consequences.

Like Hull, counsel made no mention of explanations given in parliament, and ignored important aspects of the legislation:

- the restriction on membership of the syllabus conference to those religions and denominations present in the area

- the positive provisions for withdrawal in the legislation, arguing instead that a need to avoid withdrawals (nowhere stated in statute) meant that religious education must not urge any particular belief upon pupils

- the provision for a plurality of syllabuses to take account of different beliefs.

In taking this view, counsel relied partly on the prohibition of teaching by means of denominational formularies. But this was to leave out of account the fact that some teaching was to be given 'by means of' something else, implying that this teaching carried a degree of authority. This teaching was always understood to be non-denominational Christianity. Counsel appeared to have no knowledge of the meaning given to the law by those promoting it within parliament. To an extent this may be explained by the fact that up till 1993 it was customary for judges not to make use of *Hansard* in interpreting statute.[33] Counsel therefore would have relied upon his own judgment and that of expert witnesses in 1991. However, there were witnesses, such as Cox and Cairns or the Campaign for Real Education, who could have alerted him to a different view. The opinion of counsel has been enormously influential yet it was never tested in court where its inadequacies might have been revealed.

The SCAA Model Syllabuses

Armed with counsel's opinion, civil servants felt confident that they could work on the basis that the law now required all the principal religions to be taught. The Department began to receive complaints from LEAs who were concerned that they did not have the money to provide the necessary expertise to produce teaching on all the religions now stated (three years after the event) to be required by law. In response the Government funded working parties from the six religions, under the supervision of the Schools Curriculum and Assessment Authority (SCAA), to produce model syllabuses which would set out what these faith communities wanted children to learn of their religions.

Baroness Blatch was at the DES[34] between 1992 and 1994 and experienced serious conflict with civil servants there when working on the SCAA models. She was told repeatedly that the law required all principal religions to be taught and her wish to give advice about teaching Christianity with conviction was resisted at every turn. She would write a section and have it returned to her, altered. She would try again and the same thing would happen.

The DfEE's Misquoting Of The Law On RE

When the model syllabuses were published the department quoted the words about not urging a particular religion or religious belief, first used by counsel in the Ealing case, as if these words were contained in section 26 of the 1944 Education Act.[35] Educational consultant Fred Naylor[36] pointed this out to the Department and after a lengthy correspondence and much determination on the part of Naylor, the mistake was corrected and a letter sent to all SACREs in England informing them of the mistake. It was stated, however, that it was still the view of the Department that syllabuses must not urge a particular religion or religious belief upon pupils. In support, the same section 26 of the 1944 Act was given. It seemed that the Department at this point felt confident that while this section of the law did not specifically prohibit such 'urging', it could be used in support of the view that urging a particular religion or religious belief was against the law.

Fred Naylor was certain that this was wrong and a case came up in 1997 which proved him to be right. A parent from the Isle of Wight had complained to the Department for Education and Employment (DfEE) that the syllabus was urging 'New Age' beliefs upon his child. The DfEE wrote to Mr Naylor saying that the complaint had to be rejected since the law did not prohibit the urging of beliefs upon pupils: '*no* religious beliefs urged on pupils would fall foul of section 376 (2) of the 1996 Act'.[37] The same letter stated that it was the view of the department that, although not a statutory requirement, the nature of religious education was such that it should not urge a religious belief upon pupils.

To this day, the DfEE stands by its view of the nature of religious education and has refused to alter its advice contained in official documents. Paragraph 32 of Circular 1/9 states:

> Syllabuses must not be designed to convert pupils, or to urge a particular religion or religious belief upon pupils.[38]

Section 26 of the 1944 Act (now section 376 [2] of the 1996 Act) is still quoted in support of this statement. Yet the Department has stated categorically that this section of the law does not prohibit a syllabus that urges religious beliefs upon pupils. If the law allows something, is it right for the department to forbid it? The DfEE should make it clear to all SACREs that the advice they are giving is not a legal requirement, and is not supported by law. The reference to section 26 should be rescinded since, on the Department's own admission, it does not prohibit the urging of a religious belief upon pupils.

Conclusion

What we have is a situation where the will of parliament has been frustrated and we are left with an outcome diametrically opposed to that intended by the legislators in 1988. In a democratic society this cannot be a desirable outcome.

The RE profession found itself in a situation where it was able to create, implement, and insist on, a quite contrary view of the law. But there was always the worry that the original intention might be reinstated. Between 1988 and 1996 the editor of the *BJRE* argued the case for the interpretation he himself had created; indeed such was his concern that his editorials addressed little else. An article in the *BJRE* in 1991,[39] three years after the event, gave a blow by blow account of the debates in the House of Lords which managed to omit entirely the explanation given by the Bishop of London, despite being written by Colin Alves, his officer at the Board of Education.

What of the outcome in schools? The view that an agreed syllabus must include all the principal religions *and* reflect local concerns has led, in the case of Liverpool Education Authority, to a situation where nine religions are taught to children between the ages of five and 16. Across the country it is the norm for children to learn at least six religions. It is often the case that Christianity takes up at least 50 per cent of the teaching time[40] which means that the other religions have to be fitted into the remaining time, a mere ten per cent or less for each religion. There will be pressure from other religions to be included as 'principal'. Indeed the Prime Minister recently invited representatives from nine religions to a conference, thus giving a view as to the principal religions of the country. All these will now have to be taught if one follows the guidance of Circular 1/94 that 'all the principal religions must be included'. There is limited time for RE. Would anyone seriously attempt to teach five languages *and* English to school-age children?

It is a surprising fact that only one empirical study has attempted to assess the effectiveness of a religious education that teaches the number of religions now generally taught. This study showed that pupils who learned more than four religions were more likely to get confused than those who had studied two or three religions.[41] The outcome in terms of how our children are taught religious education may be in some respects worse than it was prior to 1988.

The repeated view of officialdom that religious education must not 'urge a particular religion or religious belief' upon pupils has meant that it is likely that nothing of a religious nature will be taught to pupils with any authority or conviction. One may not urge the love of God, nor the love of neighbour, neither the avoidance of vice nor the pursuit of virtue. Care must be taken lest pupils receive the impression that they are being urged to obey their parents or to refrain from promiscuity. To the extent that a religion urges examination of conscience, love of beauty or care of animals, so must a teacher beware lest such precepts be taught as if they were true. But, it might be noted, nothing is said to prohibit secular beliefs being urged upon pupils and taught as if they were true. So the teacher would be entirely justified in insisting upon such secular insights as the absurdity of all religions, the mythical status of religious beliefs, the fact that the universe has come about by chance and the non-reality of God. Or it may be that the conscientious teacher (and let us not forget that means most) feels that somehow nothing should be urged on pupils as true. So it happens that the teacher urges (for that is what a teacher does whether realising it or not) the children to set themselves up as the final authority by listening to their own imperial selves. Pupils themselves, the conscientious teacher urges, must be the arbiters of what is true and lovely with no interference from her to assault or contaminate their thought processes. And so it comes about that she alone, of all teachers in the school, has no wisdom to impart. The fear of the Lord was once thought to be the beginning of wisdom; prohibiting the fear of the Lord has brought about the abandonment of wisdom.

It is the greatest tragedy that religious education has, to an extent, been reduced to this. And yet it need not and should not have happened. The real meaning of the law has been obscured so successfully that few know it and fewer still attempt to follow it. In its place the liberal establishment has ordained a form of religious education that was specifically rejected by parliament. This needs to be exposed. SACREs and agreed syllabus conferences need to know what the real intention of the law was so that they can begin to provide a different sort of religious education; one which proceeds 'by means of' a particular faith, thus laying the foundation for real spiritual growth. The matter ought at least to be debated. At present many within the profession resist such a debate.

Notes

Foreword

1 Archbishops' Council Church Schools Review Group, *The Way Ahead: Church of England schools in the new millennium*, (Dearing Report), London: Church House Publishing, 2001, p. 1, 1:3.

2 Department for Education and Employment (DfEE), *Schools: Building on Success* (green paper), London: DfEE, 12 February 2001.

3 Church Schools Review Group, *The Way Ahead*, 2001, p. 3, 3:25.

4 Church Schools Review Group, *The Way Ahead*, 2001, p. 15, 3:26.

5 Church Schools Review Group, *The Way Ahead*, 2001, p. 20, 4:6.

6 Church Schools Review Group, *The Way Ahead*, 2001, p. 42, 5:28.

Introduction

1 Archbishops' Council Church Schools Review Group, *The Way Ahead: Church of England schools in the new millennium*, (Dearing Report), London: Church House Publishing, 2001.

2 It is the policy of CIVITAS Education Unit to underpin arguments, wherever possible, with information about the actual standards of achievement of schools and pupils and, where such information exists, to present analyses for all the pupils in the country.

3 For further discussion see Marks, J., *An Anatomy of Failure: Standards in English Schools for 1997*, London: Social Market Foundation, 1998; and Marks, J., *The Betrayed Generations*, London: Centre for Policy Studies, 2001.

4 For further discussion see the reports cited in note 3 above together with Marks, J., *Standards of English & Maths in Primary Schools for 1995*, London: Social Market Foundation, 1996; *Standards of Arithmetic: How to Correct the Decline*, London: Centre for Policy Studies, 1996; *Standards of Reading, Spelling & Maths*

for 7-year-olds in Primary Schools for 1995, London: Social Market Foundation, 1997; *A Selective or Comprehensive System: Which Works Best?* London: Centre for Policy Studies, 1998; *Value for Money in LEA Schools*, London: Centre for Policy Studies, 1998; *What are Special Educational Needs?*, London: Centre for Policy Studies, 2000.

Standards in Church of England, Roman Catholic and LEA schools in England

1 It would clearly be useful if comparisons could easily be made between the prior attainment of pupils when they enter a school and the results they achieve when they leave it—for example, by comparing average Key Stage 2 results at 11 with GCSE results in secondary schools, or average Key Stage 1 results at seven with Key Stage 2 results at 11 for primary schools. Such prior attainment data could easily be collected annually from every school, using form 7 which is completed by each school in January each year and sent to the DfEE, and published in national performance tables alongside the results of pupils as they leave the school. The result would be that the current unreliable indicator used by the DfEE, QCA and Ofsted to differentiate between the intake of pupils in different schools—the proportion of pupils either eligible for, or taking up, free school meals—could be abandoned. This would be highly desirable; the free school meals indicator is unreliable because the data is collected in different ways in different schools and LEAs and is, in any case, much less highly correlated with standards and achievement than is prior attainment.

2 Most of the national curriculum and GCSE results given in this section are for 1998; this does not detract from the importance of this data because the characteristics of any modern education system do not change much from one year to the next or even over a five-year period.

3 'Subject ages' are calculated from the average national curriculum level for each school using the relationship 'Age' = (3 + 2*average level). The expected level for 11 year olds is Level 4; if all pupils were at this level, the 'subject age' would be (3 + 2*4) = 11. National

curriculum levels, and the related government targets
for various ages, are not arbitrary; they are based on a
national curriculum which was arrived at after wide
consultation and on the input of many experienced
HMIs and other experts. National curriculum tests go
through many stages of development in which teachers
and other subject experts are consulted: see, for
example *Weighing the Baby: The report of the
Independent Scrutiny Panel on the 1999 Key Stage 2
National Curriculum tests in English and mathematics*,
July 1999, DfEE.

4   For more detail on the data in Sections 1.1 and 1.2 see
Marks, J., *An Anatomy of Failure: Standards in
English Schools for 1997*, London: Social Market
Foundation, 1998. and *The Betrayed Generations:
Standards in British Schools 1950-2000*, London:
Centre for Policy Studies, 2001.

5   GCSE points are calculated by allocating 8 points for
an A*; 7 points for an A; 6 points for a B down to 2
points for an F; and 1 point for a grade G.

6   A-Level points are calculated by allocating 10 points to
an A, 8 points to a B, 6 points to a C, 4 points to a D and
2 points to an E; a higher average points score
therefore means a larger share of the higher grades.

7   For further discussion see Marks, J., *An Anatomy of
Failure: Standards in English Schools for 1997,*
London: Social Market Foundation, 1998; and Marks,
J., *The Betrayed Generations*, London: Centre for Policy
Studies, 2001.

8   For further discussion see the reports cited in note 7
above together with Marks, J., *Standards of English &
Maths in Primary Schools for 1995,* London: Social
Market Foundation, 1996; *Standards of Arithmetic:
How to correct the decline,* London: Centre for Policy
Studies, 1996; *Standards of Reading, Spelling & Maths
for 7-year olds in Primary Schools for 1995*, London:
Social Market Foundation, 1997; *A Selective or
Comprehensive System: which works best?,* London:
Centre for Policy Studies, 1998; *Value for Money in
LEA Schools,* London: Centre for Policy Studies, 1998;
What are Special Educational Needs?, London: Centre
for Policy Studies, 2000.

Church Schools: A Critique of Much Current Practice

1 For further discussion see Pilkington, P., 'The Church in Education', essay in this publication; and Dennis, N., *The Uncertain Trumpet*, London: Civitas, 2001.

The Church in Education

1 Newsome, D., *Godliness and Good Learning*, John Murray, 1961.

2 Archbishops' Council Church Schools Review Group, *The Way Ahead: Church of England schools in the new millennium*, (Dearing Report), London: Church House Publishing, 2001, p. 7.

3 *Future in Partnership*, National Society, 1984.

4 Church Schools Review Group, *The Way Ahead*, 2001, p. 47, para. 6.17.

How the Will of Parliament on Religious Education was Diluted by Civil Servants and the Religious Education Profession

1 House of Lords Official Report (*Hansard*), 21 June 1988, col. 717.

2 House of Lords Official Report (*Hansard*), 21 June 1988, col. 720.

3 House of Lords Official Report (*Hansard*), 21 June 1988, col. 721.

4 This provision was taken over from the 1944 Education Act.

5 Whereas the SACRE may co-opt members.

6 House of Commons, *Hansard*, 23 March 1988, col. 421.

7 The *Independent*, 22 June 1988.

8 *British Journal of Religious Education*, Autumn, 1988 pp. 1 and 2.

9 The REC is a forum for discussion and joint action in the field of religious education in England and Wales. Membership of the council is confined to corporate bodies which have a national interest in the teaching of the subject.

10 *Religious Education and Collective Worship*, Circular 3/89, p. 35.

11 This is a modification of the Cowper Temple clause which had been in place since the 1870 Act.

12 *Religious Education and Collective Worship*, p. 35.

13 *Religious Education and Collective Worship*, para. 34, p. 37.

14 A determination is a decision made by a SACRE to allow a school to be freed from the requirement to conduct worship of a broadly Christian nature. A school must apply to a SACRE who will consider the family backgrounds of the pupils when deciding whether or not to allow the determination.

15 Personal interview with Rev. G. Miller, 11 June 2000.

16 'Each agreed syllabus must recognise the other religions which are practised in its area', Taylor, M.J., *Religious Education Values and Worship: LEA Advisers' Perspectives on Implementation of the Education Reform Act 1988*, National Foundation for Educational Research and Religious Education Council, May 1989, p. 28.

17 Hull, J., *The Act Unpacked*, The University of Birmingham and CEM, 1989, p. 14.

18 'Teaching Religious Education', *Education Digest*, 18 November 1988, p. ii.

19 *BJRE*, Vol. 11, No. 2, Spring 1989, p. 61.

20 *Handbook for Agreed Syllabus Conferences, SACREs and Schools*, the report of a working party of the Religious Education Council of England and Wales, 1989, p. 5.

21 *Reforming Religious Education: the religious clauses of the ERA*, Cox, E. and Cairns, J., London: Kogan Page, 1989.

22 Cox and Cairns' view was that the 'taking account of' phrase, by being cast in a subordinate clause, had caused offence to minorities and that section 8 (3) was really about undergirding Christian faith in the majority of pupils. Cox and Cairns make no mention of the explanation given in parliament.

23 Bradney, A., 'The Dewsbury Affair and RE', *Education and the Law*, Vol. 1, Part 2, 1989, p. 57.

24 Harte, J.D.C., 'The religious dimension of the Education Reform Act 1988', *Ecclesiastical Law Journal*, Issue 5, 1989, p. 36.

25 Harte, 'The religious dimension of the Education Reform Act 1988', 1989, p. 37.

26 *Acts of Worship and Religious Education*, CRE, 1990, Helpsheet no. 9.

27 The offices of the National Society are at Church House, Great Smith Street, London, SW1 2NZ.

28 *Religious Education*, National Society, 1989.

29 Circular 3/89, quoting Schedule 5 of the 1944 Education Act as amended by the 1988 ERA, states: 'where the LEA propose to adopt more than one syllabus of religious education for use in schools maintained by them, the authority shall inform the conference as to the schools in which, or in the case of a syllabus intended to be used by certain pupils only, the class or description of pupils for which the syllabus prepared by the conference is to be used.' Annex E p. 61.

30 See article by Alves, C., 'Just a matter of words? The Religious Education Debate in the House of Lords', *BJRE*, Vol. 13, No. 3, Summer 1991, p. 168. See also *Forum for the Discussion of New Trends in Education*, Vol. 32, No. 2, Spring 1990, where there are several articles defending the new interpretation.

31 The phrase used by the barrister in his opinion. This opinion is the property of the DfEE.

32 This information was given to me by John Hull.

33 This was the case of Pepper *vs* Hart, 1993. This case concerned an ambiguity in the wording of a law relating to the payment of tax by teachers whose children were receiving subsidised education at the private school where they were employed. The matter hinged on the admissibility or otherwise of the explanations of the law to be found in *Hansard*. The Law Lords judged that where an ambiguous wording was given a clear explanation by a promoter of the Bill in the parliamentary record, that explanation should

be accepted as the true meaning. What this means is that in interpreting the law, an agreed syllabus conference should accept the explanation of section 8 (3) given in parliament. It is in fact *because* the wording is ambiguous that conferences should take note of the explanation given by the legislators. Pepper *vs* Hart has had considerable effect in legal judgments ever since 1993.

34 As under secretary of state for education under the Conservatives.

35 'The Education Act (1944) requires that an agreed syllabus "must not be designed to convert pupils, or to urge a particular religion or religious belief on pupils" (Education Act 1944, section 26 (2).' *Religious Education*, SCAA, Model Syllabuses: Model 1 Living Faiths Today, 1994.

36 Mr Naylor is honorary secretary of the Parental Alliance for Choice in Education (PACE).

37 Letter to Mr Naylor, dated 25 March, 1997 from C. Drury of the Curriculum and Assessment Division of the DfEE (emphasis in the original). Section 376 (2) of the 1996 Act replaces section 26 of the 1944 Act.

38 This circular is still in force. It was written to follow the 1993 Education Act and has largely followed the view of counsel, despite the Government of the day seeking to rein in the profession and reinstate the view of the Act found in the debates of 1988.

39 Alves, 'Just a matter of words?', 1991.

40 In order to make sense of the requirement to reflect the fact that the religious traditions of the country are 'in the main Christian'.

41 This was a study of more than 2,500 secondary pupils in 22 co-educational comprehensive schools in England. The same study sounded a warning about the thematic study of religions (akin to mishmash) showing that pupils who were taught this way had a less positive attitude to religions than those who had been taught each religion systematically. See Kay, W. and Smith, L., 'Religious Terms and Attitudes in the Classroom', Parts 1 and 2, *BJRE*, Spring and Summer 2000, Vols. 22, 2 and 22, 3.